NEW DIRECTIONS FOR TEACHING AND LEARNING

Robert E. Young, *University of Wisconsin*
EDITOR-IN-CHIEF

The Changing Face of College Teaching

Marilla D. Svinicki
University of Texas,
POD Network in Higher Education

EDITOR

Number 42, Summer 1990

JOSSEY-BASS INC., PUBLISHERS
San Francisco • Oxford

The Changing Face of College Teaching.
Marilla D. Svinicki (ed.).
New Directions for Teaching and Learning, no. 42.

NEW DIRECTIONS FOR TEACHING AND LEARNING
Robert E. Young, Editor-in-Chief

NEW DIRECTIONS FOR TEACHING AND LEARNING is part of The
Jossey-Bass Higher Education Series and is published quarterly
by Jossey-Bass Inc., Publishers. Second-class postage paid at San
Francisco, California, and at additional mailing offices. Postmaster:
Send address changes to Jossey-Bass Inc., Publishers, 350 Sansome
Street, San Francisco, California 94104.

EDITORIAL CORRESPONDENCE should be sent to the Editor-in-Chief,
Robert E. Young, Dean, University of Wisconsin Center, Fox Valley,
1478 Midway Rd., Menasha, Wisconsin 54952.

Library of Congress Catalog Card Number LC 85-644763

International Standard Serial Number ISSN 0271-0633

International Standard Book Number ISBN 1-55542-839-8

Cover photograph by Richard Blair/Color & Light © 1990.

Manufactured in the United States of America. Printed on acid-free paper.

CONTENTS

PART Two: Changing Perspectives

Editor's Notes

It has been suggested (Cross, 1989) that the greatest educational reform will come not through the sweeping changes of large, institutionally mandated programs but through the small, day-to-day improvements that faculty members make in their own courses. The faculty is the first line of revolution in teaching; without their cooperation, no change is possible; with it, no challenge is impossible.

Yet, these already overworked individuals seldom have the time or training to keep up with all the instructional innovations their colleagues are exploring or with the newest findings in educational research, were they so inclined to explore them. There is a real need for "translators and disseminators" whose job it is to extract the best from the array of potential ideas and pass it along in workable form to individual faculty members. When this volume was conceived, the series editor approached just such a group of individuals (the Professional and Organizational Development Network in Higher Education) and asked them to search their collective wisdom for ideas about teaching that would be of special value and interest to faculty members and to collect and translate those ideas in such a way as to make them accessible to others. The chapter authors are faculty members as well as faculty and instructional developers and are therefore cognizant of the problems that arise when we attempt to translate the ideal to the reality of the classroom. Each has tried to strike a balance between the two by providing both the model and its practical application.

The volume begins with descriptions of teaching possibilities that the reader can adapt to his or her own class, but which represent significant changes in the way one would think about the face of college teaching. In the past, teaching has always been equated with telling; and improving teaching meant thinking of better ways to present information. The methods discussed in the initial chapters represent a change in that definition, reflecting the change in what we now know about how learning best occurs. Viewed from that perspective, the methods described are not in fact different methods of teaching but rather facets of the same reformation, the move to active involvement in learning by students.

In Part One, MacGregor describes the tenets of collaborative learning, in which students work with each other to learn jointly, resulting in significant changes in some of the more forward thinking institutions. Tomlinson reviews the bases and status of the recent push to increase the amount of writing in classes of all types. She explores the philosophy behind the movement and why its current problems may be the result of deviations from the original philosophy. Boehrer and Linsky take a very thorough look at the case method, an old approach to teaching which is making new inroads in colleges and universities that are trying to teach complex analytic skills in the face of an exploding information base. Finally, Peters gives a glimpse of the changes in teaching that result from a changing student population and a philosophical shift from "education as selection" to "education as facilitation." He discusses the supplemental instruction concept and how individual instructors can implement it in their classrooms.

In Part Two, the volume shifts to a series of chapters that encourage faculty to take a more proactive, inquiry-oriented approach to their classes. Angelo begins the series by suggesting that a focus on what and how students are learning through the use of continuous classroom assessment will have a large impact on an instructor's ability to improve the quality of instruction, regardless of what teaching method is used. Pintrich and Johnson and Janzow and Eison describe instruments that the instructor can administer to find out who is in his or her classes and what strengths, weaknesses, and attitudes drive those students. On the basis of such information, the instructor may be able to modify the instructional methods to match the needs of the students more effectively. Lucas suggests that the instructor can become more scholarly in his or her approach to teaching by understanding and using models of human behavior that explain and predict the factors influencing students' responses to classroom teaching. These models can then be used to generate new methods for motivating students.

Finally, the last chapter deals with the next steps. Weimer provides an analysis of the kinds of materials and resources available to help instructors keep up with changes in instructional practice and theory, so that they can become self-renewing teachers.

Marilla D. Svinicki
Editor

Reference

Cross, K. P. *Reforming Undergraduate Education One Class at a Time.* Teaching Excellence Series. Honolulu, Hawaii: Professional and Organizational Development Network in Higher Education, 1989.

Marilla D. Svinicki is the director of the Center for Teaching Effectiveness at the University of Texas, Austin, and a past executive director of the Professional and Organizational Development Network in Higher Education, the group responsible for the contents of this volume. The POD Network is an association of individuals at colleges and universities across the United States and Canada who have an interest in or responsibility for faculty or instructional development on their campuses.

Bringing the process of creative thinking to the act of changing teaching offers several alternatives for ways in which instructors can look at their own methods. But change should always be approached with caution, lest it overwhelm the instructor.

Changing the Face of *Your* Teaching

Marilla D. Svinicki

Anyone who thinks that all you need in order to teach is knowledge of course content has missed the boat. Knowing your content is only the first step toward teaching: a necessary step, but still just a first step. Teaching is more than understanding; it is helping others understand. That requires understanding "the others" and understanding "understanding." All the sophisticated content knowledge in the world is not of much use to anyone if it cannot be communicated. Therefore, learning more about your content will not automatically make you a better teacher; you must understand and change the face of your teaching itself. The goal of this chapter is to suggest some ways to make that change without completely overwhelming yourself in the process.

Changing by Adapting Ideas from Others

One of the advantages of a volume like this is that it provides a variety of alternative ideas that can be adapted to a local situation. As is mentioned in the final chapter on resources, you keep up with what is current not because all of the ideas you come across will fit neatly into your course but rather because they serve as basic templates that can be modified according to the course, content, student, and instructor variables of a given class. The more variations with which you are familiar, the more alternatives you will have in your repertoire to solve the continually changing problems you face in teaching.

For example, the idea of using writing as a tool for learning may seem strange in the context of a course on computer programming, but brief writing episodes to document program ideas can not only help stu-

NEW DIRECTIONS FOR TEACHING AND LEARNING, no. 42, Summer 1990 © Jossey-Bass Inc., Publishers

dents be more exact in their thinking about programming but also might provide an alternative mode of thinking for students who have difficulty imagining program structures from code alone. If you stop thinking about writing as an end in itself and begin to recognize the value of writing as a means to learning, the instructional possibilities become much clearer. Thus, the *idea* of writing can be used even if traditional writing assignments or extensive editing of student writing are inappropriate for your class.

Or take the example of collaborative learning. Most instructors envision an elaborate group-project process by which students work together to design large-scale presentations or position papers. But the idea of collaborative learning is much simpler than that. It simply means opportunities for students to work together on common problems. The problems might take only five minutes to solve, but there is still collaboration.

This process of adapting the ideas of others is one of the techniques of creative thinking. It involves winnowing an idea down to its basic components and then rebuilding it in a new form to fit the demands of the situation. For example, what is a pencil anyway? It could be viewed as a holder for lead; would some other receptacle for lead be as useful in a different setting? It might be viewed as a device to make marks; what other system could be used to make marks? The chapter on supplemental instruction in this volume is essentially an adaptation from a much more elaborate system. Would an adaptation of that adaptation work for your class?

The message here is, first, to be on the lookout for new ideas for your classes by sampling a lot of different sources. Several ideas and sources are described in this volume, but you are surrounded by other sources every day. There are your colleagues. Surely their teaching differs from yours in some respects. Are any of their ideas adaptable? You have to ask about their teaching in order to find out, a process not widespread in many institutions, particularly with respect to cross-department interaction among instructors. However, you can learn a great deal about your own teaching if you sit in on someone else's classes and look beyond the specifics of the content.

You can get ideas from outside the institution as well. There are some very effective teaching strategies (or at least communication strategies) on display all around us, on television, in printed matter, in museums and stores, and in the way information is packaged for rapid consumption by business executives and other busy consumers. Much as we hate to admit it, our students are consumers of our content; is there anything we can learn from everyday experience that will make them better consumers of our offerings? Of course, there is. For example, visual enhancements, summaries, contrasting ideas, the surprise or suspense factor as a motivator, and humor are all used constantly in communicating with the public and make just as much sense when we think about ways to communicate with our students.

So one of the ways of changing your teaching is to become sensitive to ideas about teaching that can be adapted to your classes from a variety of sources. And another is to become facile at extracting the essence of ideas rather than focusing on the specifics of particular examples. For example, it is not the specific use of supplemental instruction on test-taking skills that is the point; rather, it is that there are skills required of each class that may not be in students' repertoires but could be developed if the instructor made them explicit and provided some instruction about them. It is not the full-blown case study that needs to be incorporated into your class but instead the idea that students are both motivated and helped to understanding when we provide concrete contexts for abstract principles and allow them to actively work to solve problems rather than passively receive the solutions in a lecture.

Changing by Looking from New Perspectives

Another way to change the face of your teaching is to look at it from a different perspective. This is another technique of creative thinking: view an objective from a different perspective in order to discover aspects of it that are hidden from view.

Several of the chapters in this volume encourage you to consider a different perspective on teaching. They ask you to stop viewing teaching as "covering the content" and to start viewing it as "helping the students learn." The implications of this change are great. As MacGregor (Chapter 2) puts it, we are asking you to "reframe" the roles of both teacher and student.

One change in teaching viewed from this perspective is that the focus of the class is the student, not the content. The classroom becomes a place for students to get involved in learning rather than being passive observers of the ongoing scene. We are encouraged to turn some of the work over to the students rather than to take total responsibility for what goes on every minute in the classroom. In collaborative learning, case studies, and writing, the students must tackle the act of learning themselves; the instructor guides the process but does not give "the answer." When you release yourself from the responsibility of providing all the instruction in a class and accept that students can learn a lot on their own or from their peers in a well-designed course, you will be amazed at what a different face that gives to the classroom. When you add the idea that students learn from failures as well as successes, that they can learn by watching someone else (including you) try to solve a difficult puzzle, even more of the pressure to be "right" and "perfect" is removed; teaching becomes an act of mutual learning rather than a one-person show.

Viewing teaching from the perspective of the students also implies that we benefit from knowing more about what students think and what they are like. Three of the chapters (7, 8, and 9) deal with this concept. Understanding how our students go about grappling with new information—how they organize it, store it, recall it, and manage it—can help us design ways to complement their normal methods or can help us help them to be more effective in these tasks. Understanding whether they have a predominantly learning orientation or grade orientation can increase our tolerance of student values and attitudes that are different from our own. Understanding what motivates students and how they develop cognitively and emotionally can help us remember back to what it was like "not to know" so that we can be more tolerant and more creative in helping them bridge the gap between novice learner and expert.

There are lots of other perspectives from which we might view our teaching. For example, the perspective of the person who teaches the previous course in the sequence or the next course in the sequence might be very informative. Do we even know what that person thinks is going on in our classes? Do we know what goes on in his or her classes? Angelo, in Chapter 6, cites the example of a group of engineering faculty members who discovered that they all had very different ideas about the goals of a common course. Different goals lead to very different instructional practices. If you changed the goals of your course to match those of other constituencies, what would be the effects on the class and how it was conducted?

Changing Through the Use of Models

A very effective generative technique for changing teaching is the use of models to suggest alternatives. A number of models are presented in this book, any one of which can be used to stimulate your thinking on how instruction might be done differently. The use of models, however, requires a willingness to play with ideas and to order one's thinking rather than to apply "hit or miss" or "it's always done this way" methods of thinking about teaching.

Models are best used to suggest and order possibilities where you might not have considered them. For example, a very simple yet powerful model for instructional design is presented in Figure 1. It is based on Kolb's (1981) experiential learning cycle, which proposes that learning moves through four phases: experience, reflection, abstraction, and experimentation. This characterization of learning is not a profoundly complex idea; it very much reflects the scientific method in general and the active learning techniques supported early on by Dewey, Lewin, and others. Its value as a heuristic for instructional design is very strong, however. If an instructor chooses one activity that leads to each of the four points on the circle, designing novel instructional sequences or adapting new methods to the class becomes much easier. For example, we begin by having the students *experience* some concrete phenomena, such as in the laboratory. They are then asked to *reflect* in groups about what they have observed, compare it to what others have observed, or to their own past experiences; perhaps they are even asked to write a short essay describing their observations and speculating on what they have seen. Each small group is asked to come up with an explanation that *abstracts* a general principle from the observations they have made and makes a prediction about what might happen in a different situation. Finally, they return to the laboratory to test their abstraction with an *experiment.* The results of that experiment then become the experiences for the next round of learning.

Figure 1. The Experiential Learning Cycle

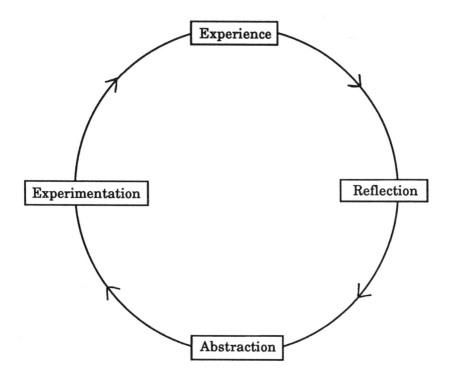

Source: Adapted from Kolb, 1981.

This simple model can be used to design instructional sequences for all manner of content (see Svinicki and Dixon, 1987). Its advantage is that the four phases force the instructor to think of possible ways of incorporating each phase into his or her content. What does it mean to experience in a history class, for example? You cannot experience history. Or can you? Would seeing news clips about World War II provide some observational experience? How about interviewing grandparents? Or reading original journals of pioneers? How does one reflect in a math class? Would a writing exercise in which the students tried to describe how they went about solving a problem cause them to reflect on what they did? How about comparing different problem solutions and analyzing how different students approached the same problem? Or one might have the students compare different problems that are actually different versions of the same basic process.

From these few examples, you can see that using a model such as Kolb's can spark your thinking about how you might achieve each phase of the cycle. The model also forces the instructor to think more carefully about what is actually going on in the methods currently in use. For example, in a lecture, are the students *experiencing?* Not in the sense intended by Kolb; they are not experiencing the actual phenomenon. Are they *reflecting* on their experience? Possibly, if we ask a lot of questions and give them time to think. Are they *abstracting* general principles? Well, they are not doing it, but they are observing someone else doing it so that is probably one of the functions of lectures. Are they *experimenting* with or testing those abstractions? Probably not; they have to learn them first. Actually, Svinicki and Dixon (1987) have expanded this model along another dimension, that of active participation, and accounted for even more of our traditional teaching methods.

Before you rush out to try one of the teaching methods suggested in this volume, you might want to clarify for yourself to what phase of learning each would most contribute in your class. For example, writing is probably best used as a reflection tool, forcing students to think about their observations and put those thoughts into words. However, the examination of samples of writing for analysis can serve as the basis for observation, much like laboratory experiments in the sciences. Or, if the student has been studying a particular model of writing, a writing assignment in which that model is applied would be tapping the experimentation phase. Case studies can take the students through all four phases. The case materials themselves serve as experience instances; writing up the case forces reflection; discussion of the case supports, first, reflection and then abstraction as the conclusions are reached. Cases can also be analyzed against preset models to see if the models apply in reality, and therefore through the cases students can experiment with or apply what they have learned. Collaborative learning is probably most useful in the reflection and abstraction phases, although group work provides more opportunities and possibilities for breadth of observation of experience as well.

You can see from this example that models are a very useful source of ideas to change your teaching. The chapters in this volume offer some interesting models which can be used to order your thinking about teaching. Lucas describes several models of human behavior that are particularly valuable. For example, if we use the cognitive developmental models she discusses, we can think about what kinds of problems will be challenging to our students at different times in their academic careers, and what kinds of support students will need along the way.

Another example of a model that can guide instructional practice is the expectancy-value model Lucas discusses. By identifying the components of motivation that affect student effort, the model pinpoints areas where we can and cannot intervene. For example, we cannot change the fact that students come to our classes equipped with certain skills but lacking others, which will affect their probability of success (although, as Peters suggests, we might be able to help them develop skills appropriate to our course). However, we can manipulate our assignments to take advantage of the skills they currently have while still helping them to develop those they need. This teaching strategy will allow them some measure of control over the task of learning and increase their expectancy for success while still maintaining the challenge of learning. Because of this model we also recognize the importance of making the tasks sufficiently challenging so as to instill pride at their successful completion. Completion of a simple task, while valuable, is not nearly as satisfying as completion of a more challenging task. However, a task that is too difficult to complete lacks motivational value.

The models behind the learning orientation/grade orientation approach (LOGO) in Janzow and Eison's chapter and the Motivated Strategies for Learning Questionnaire (MSLQ) in Pintrich and Johnson's chapter are equally interesting as sources of change in teaching. The two models challenge the instructor to think about how students attack learning, what drives their performance, and consequently what can be done to improve performance. Janzow and Eison also provide a model for evaluating the instructor's attitudes and behavior and the congruence between them.

These are, of course, not the only models of significance to teaching. In fact, as instructors, we approach our task with implicit models of teaching that drive our classroom choices (Menges and Rando, 1989). Making these models explicit often helps us understand ourselves and our choices, which is the driving force behind the "reflective practitioner" movement (Schön, 1987). The consideration of new models is a way of changing our teaching in creative ways.

Changing by Inquiry

Whether we adapt the techniques of others or generate new ones by taking different perspectives and considering different models, we should adopt an attitude toward teaching that is as inquiry-oriented as the attitude we each have toward our respective disciplines. No scholar worthy of the title would be caught conducting the same experiment year after year without examining and modifying the paradigm and procedures to improve the results or extend what is learned from them. Nor would that person take pride in never having read a book or article in the field. Scholars approach their work with an attitude of questioning, an excitement of exploration, and a dedication to staying on the cutting edge of their particular disciplines. The application of that attitude of inquiry to teaching can advance our personal understanding of the process almost as rapidly as we advance our disciplines. As Angelo points out in his chapter, we should be engaged in classroom assessment of our students' learning on a daily basis, both to insure that learning is taking place and to support a questioning attitude toward teaching. We should be curious about what is happening on the other side of the desk, if not from a human interest point of view then from a scholarly one.

Where to Start

It is one thing to be curious in the abstract about teaching and quite another to put that sense of inquiry into practice on Monday. Where and how should instructors begin to change the face of their teaching? Here are some suggestions:

Start small. Do not take on the revision of the entire curriculum. Choose something over which you have some control, one assignment in one class, for example. Teachers are very busy people. If you try to do too much at once, you will never see the results of your efforts, and, as Lucas observes in her chapter here, expectations for success are an important factor in motivation.

You can select a new activity you want to try, such as writing, and see if there is a spot for it in your course as it now stands. Or you can select a class session, activity, evaluation procedure, or other method you already use and see if you can make it better with the use of classroom assessment procedures. Or you can simply take a closer look at what you are currently doing in order to understand it better with classroom assessment.

Find out what is already happening and what you have to work with and then make your class better. Take a close look at what is going on in your class right now. Who are your students? What are they doing in class? What are they taking away on a daily basis? Are they performing up to your expectations? This is the kind of classroom assessment recommended by Angelo, and the nature of the LOGO and MSLQ recommended by Janzow and Eison and Pintrich and Johnson, respectively. Or design a simple questionnaire or exercise that fits your own model of what or who is in your class. As was mentioned earlier, all instructors have implicit models about who is in their classes and what is happening; they just usually have not articulated them. The act of trying to gather some baseline data on your classes may bring those models to the surface for inspection.

This approach means you must have a clear picture of what is actually happening in your class. Look at the text and other materials you use. You examined them from the perspective of a professional when you chose them; now examine them from the perspective of a student. Are they comprehensible to a novice? Go the campus bookstore and look at some of the texts for other courses on topics you know nothing about. How comprehensible are they to you as a novice? Are there any that really catch your attention? What is it about them that attracts you?

Or examine one of your class sessions. Have it taped and make a transcript of what was said. Who said what? What kinds of questions were asked? Who did most of the talking? Was it interesting, organized, easy to follow? Now go observe a class in some area you know nothing about and, just as with the text, evaluate how that class comes across to a novice. Or invite someone else to come to your class to make similar observations and then get their reactions. As was mentioned in the Editor's Notes of this sourcebook, there is a whole group of individuals in the area of faculty and instructional development who make that their business. There may be a center or group on your campus who can provide that service for you.

Be clear on where you want to go. Knowing what you are starting with is one end of the process of change; knowing what you are aiming toward is the other end. If you do not know where you are going, it does not matter what route you take; but if you have a specific goal in mind, you are more likely to choose a method that will get you there—and the more specific the goal, the better. It does not suffice to say, "I want my students to participate in class more." You need to clarify what you mean by "participate." Once you have specified that, it becomes easier to design or select instructional methods that are aligned with those outcomes.

Examine the proposed change to be sure it fits what you have to work with and where you want to go. The case studies described in Chapter Four can appear promising at first glance, but they might not be right for your class if your students are not developed enough cognitively to deal with ambiguity or abstraction. If that is the case, is there some way you could modify the procedure to fit their current skill levels and still retain the essence of what is learned in case studies? If you try to implement a change that is beyond the abilities of your students, you are dooming it to failure from the start, and you may be laying the groundwork for a fear of change in the future. That is what happened to a lot of computer-assisted instruction. The appeal of the technology was huge, but the execution just did not fit the circumstances. Technology was being pursued for its own sake rather than because it fit an instructional need. So examine your proposed change in the light of your actual classroom circumstances and choose a type and level of change that is supported by your course.

Do not overanalyze or be afraid of failure. Keep in mind that this is *your* teaching you are changing, not the future of higher education. It is perfectly all right to "tinker." Things do not have to be statistically significant in order to be worthwhile; and some things that are statistically significant are still not worthwhile. At this level of inquiry, gut-level reactions are probably valid, too.

Failure should be viewed as an opportunity to learn rather than as a disaster. Always have a fall-back position, but keep the data from the failed attempt anyway because they can provide some interesting insights into what was really happening as opposed to what was supposed to happen. After all, penicillin was the result of sloppy lab work, compensated for by good observational skills and an openness to alternatives.

What to Do on Monday

Can you use any of the methods or perspectives discussed in this volume in your class on Monday? Well, not all of them, but certainly you can take five minutes at the end of class and have the students write summaries of what went on. And then you can use that writing as a classroom assessment device to see if what went on from their perspective matched what went on from yours. You might not be able to come up with a full-blown case study by Monday, but you can keep an eye out in the press for a news item that raises a discussable issue for the next few weeks. If you teach courses in which students have to apply principles to specific examples, you can initiate collaborative learning by assigning a problem in class and giving the students five minutes to talk it over with each other, even if they only get as far as figuring out what kind of solution is needed. If you have a test coming up in class, schedule a class session in which you provide supplemental instruction on how to study for and take the test. Or prepare a handout with that information if you cannot run an actual session.

Finally, become more aware of what is happening in teaching and less focused on "covering the material." Expanding your repertoire of ideas for teaching and your knowledge of resources in teaching is a good first step. Talking to others, particularly from a different discipline, is another worthwhile method of becoming more aware of the process of teaching itself, as opposed to the teaching of a specific content. Seeing how others in very different disciplines have essentially the same problems as you have and how they attempt to solve them elevates teaching to a conscious level separate from the content. If your campus has a faculty or instructional development program, the individuals connected with it should be especially helpful in extracting generalizations about teaching from specifics of discipline instruction.

But in the end it is the individual instructors who must change teaching methods, within their own classrooms and across the institution. And once the realization comes that change is possible, even if it is small, there is no stopping the revolution.

References

Kolb, D. A. "Learning Styles and Disciplinary Differences." In A. W. Chickering and Associates (eds.), *The Modern American College: Responding to the New Realities of Diverse Students and a Changing Society.* San Francisco: Jossey-Bass, 1981.

Menges, R. J., and Rando, W. C. "What Are Your Assumptions? Improving Instruction by Examining Theories." *College Teaching,* 1989, *37* (2), 54-60.

Schön, D. A. *Educating the Reflective Practitioner: Toward a New Design for Teaching and Learning in the Professions.* San Francisco: Jossey-Bass, 1987.

Svinicki, M. D., and Dixon, N. M. "The Kolb Model Modified for Classroom Activities." *College Teaching,* 1987, *35* (4), 141-146.

Marilla D. Svinicki is director of the Center for Teaching Effectiveness at the University of Texas, Austin, and a past executive director of the Professional and Organizational Development Network in Higher Education.

PART ONE

Changing Methods

Collaborative learning can unleash a unique intellectual and social synergy for teachers and students, but it requires a reframing of assumptions about the learning process and classroom roles.

Collaborative Learning: Shared Inquiry as a Process of Reform

Jean MacGregor

Having read a chapter on the origins of life in their introductory biology textbook, students arrive at class and pick up worksheets. They gather around the teacher, who, using the phospholipids in egg yolk to mix oil and water, is demonstrating hydrophobic and hydrophilic characteristics of phospholipid molecules. Then, dividing in groups of three or four, the students start on the worksheet problems. They diagram possible arrangements of phospholipids in the "primordial soup" that might have led to the first cell membranes, and then they speculate on the sources of these molecules. The teacher circulates, observing the groups and posing questions occasionally if a group appears completed stalled. The class period ends with groups sharing answers to the questions and posing additional ones of their own: fodder for the following day's discussion.

In a learning community program entitled "Revolution and Reaction," the final text for a book seminar is Hannah Arendt's *On Revolution*. Freshman students are not only able to identify important concepts such as Arendt's contrast between pity and compassion, but they are also now able to restate the essence of these concepts in simple terms, communicate them to others, and lead their peers to an understanding of them. The faculty member is struck by the students' facility at comparing Arendt's ideas to ideas raised earlier in the quarter through other assigned texts, lecture material, research paper sources, and independent reading. Flipping back and forth through the text, the students are searching for passages that help them to draw comparisons to Plato, Machiavelli, and Marx.

In a writing class organized thematically around American social history, students are working in groups to plan, draft, and polish papers. They begin by reading a brochure and viewing a video on Irish immigration to the Five Points section of New York City in the 1850s. First in small groups and then in large ones, the students discuss the content and deepen their understanding of it by creating questions for each other and answering them. Working alternately in small groups and as a whole class with the teacher, the students move through a process of brainstorming possible paper topics, which range from stereotypes and prejudice then and now to how American values were played out in the immigrant experience in New York. The students and teacher, again working in small and in large groups, move next to narrowing the list to several workable topics, discussing various rhetorical structures to achieve different goals in writing on the topics. Later, the students move to a writing lab, where they work individually at word processors, but they also circulate to read each other's material and try out ideas. After several small group work sessions on each draft, papers begin to emerge.

In each of these three situations, students and teachers are engaged in collaborative learning. Students are working with each other, and frequently alongside their teachers, to grasp subject matter or to deepen their understanding of it. In the process, they are developing their social skills, and their intellectual skills as well. Students might be interpreting, questioning, creating, synthesizing, inventing, doubting, comparing, making connections, puzzling, or doing myriad other sorts of active, visible intellectual tasks. But this active learning takes place publicly, in partnership with others. Students and their teachers are involved in a common enterprise: the *mutual* seeking of understanding. Because many minds are simultaneously grappling with the material, while working toward a common goal, collaborative learning has the potential to unleash a unique intellectual and social synergy.

There have always been social dimensions to the learning process, but only in recent decades have specially designed collaborative learning experiences been regarded as an innovative alternative to the lecture-centered and teacher-as-single-authority approaches typical of most college classrooms. Today, work on collaboration comes from a broad array of disciplines and educational philosophies, and interest in collaborative approaches is growing both inside and beyond the academy. Nevertheless, while productive, engaged communities of learners are a worthwhile ideal, the work of collaboration can be demanding for teacher and student alike.

This chapter explores some of the historical underpinnings of collaborative learning and highlights the issues involved in designing collaborative approaches. It also raises important questions for those beginning to design collaborative intellectual experiences and examines how teaching and learning in collaborative modes entails, for faculty and students, a reframing of assumptions about teachers, learners, and knowledge.

Roots of Collaboration in Education

As the 1990s begin, interest in collaborative learning has probably never been greater. This expanding work, however, is not based on a single theoretical foundation or even a very clear history of practice. The work on collaboration in education is more like an arbor of vines growing in parallel, crossing and intertwining.

Dewey, Piaget, and Vygotsky. Most of the collaborative learning vines are deeply rooted in experiential learning and student-centered instruction, the major proponents of which in this century have been philosopher John Dewey and cognitive psychologists Jean Piaget and L. S. Vygotsky. They all struggled to understand how teachers can help learners deal with the tension between what students already know (their prior experience) and what is newly presented to them. They were strong advocates of learning as experiencing. They stressed how critical it is for the teacher not simply to transmit content but also to create a context where learners can discover on their own and successfully reconstruct their understanding of the world around them. While Piaget focused on cognitive development as an individual process, Dewey and Vygotsky were convinced that learning is fundamentally social in nature.

Cooperative Learning. Many collaborative learning vines have additional roots in social psychology, particularly in the nature and power of small group theory. First articulated in the 1940s by pioneers such as Kurt Lewin and Martin Deutsch, small group theory has been applied to social interaction skills and learning in the context of team activity in workplaces and community arenas throughout the nation. Coupled with educational psychology, small group theory is in addition a principal foundation for the cooperative learning movement led by David Johnson and Roger Johnson at the University of Minnesota, and by Robert Slavin at Johns Hopkins University. This effort to develop cooperative (as opposed to competitive or individualized) goal structures for learning has developed rapidly in elementary and secondary schools. It is in this area that the most extensive evaluative research has occurred (Johnson and others, 1981; Slavin, 1983), generally corroborating the claim that students learn more in cooperative settings than they do in competitive or individualized ones.

Learning-Community Curricular Reform Efforts. Learning communities constitute another major vine in the collaborative learning arbor. This work grew out of important attempts to restructure college curricula for greater intellectual coherence and student engagement. At the University of Wisconsin in the late 1920s, philosopher Alexander Meiklejohn abandoned traditional courses in favor of an integrated, two-year, full-time program called the "Experimental College," in which students examined the classics and engaged in intensive dialogue about what it means to live in a democracy. This ground-breaking but short-lived experiment spawned several other curricular restructuring efforts, most notably Joseph Tussman's experiment at the University of California-Berkeley, St. John's and other "Great Books" colleges, and The Evergreen State College. The framers of these programs argued that the course structure itself is actually a barrier to effective learning because it abbreviates, fragments, and atomizes intellectual experience for student and professor alike. Their solution required a complete reconstruction of students' and teachers' curricular lives around full-time, integrated, interdisciplinary programs—mega-courses—usually involving both team teaching and collaborative discussion of primary texts. The threads of mutual responsibility and participation ran deep in these efforts, as they do today in expanding numbers of course-linking and curricular restructuring endeavors known as learning-community programs (Gabelnick, MacGregor, Matthews, and Smith, 1990).

Discipline-Based Efforts. Other champions of classroom collaboration have emerged in recent years from successful group work in disciplinary contexts. Kenneth Bruffee and his colleagues at the City University of New York pioneered strategies for enabling students to work on their writing—and on their thinking—out loud, with each other. This has led to a rich peer-writing approach that has transformed the writing classroom into an active workshop where, as in the real world, writers work on their writing with other writers. More recently, Uri Treisman and others at the University of California-Berkeley have revolutionized the teaching of college mathematics by developing communities of students and faculty who work together intensively.

Problem-Centered Approaches. Work in critical thinking and problem-centered learning constitutes another cluster of collaborative learning vines. Harvard University's Case Method, the work in Guided Design, McMaster University's problem-centered curricula, and a large array of home-grown simulations and "worksheet workshops"; all of these approaches involve carefully designed small group experiences. They ask teams of students to embark on tasks that challenge them to apply the ideas or practice the work of the discipline, with their teachers serving as coaches or providers of expert feedback.

Collaboration in Undergraduate Education. During the 1980s, several informal networks with interests in collaborative learning have emerged in higher education. With support and recognition from organizations such as the Fund for the Improvement of Postsecondary Education (FIPSE), the American Association of Colleges, and the American Association for Higher Education, Collaboration in Undergraduate Education

(CUE) is a network of individuals with interests not only in collaborative learning in the classroom but also in the broader issues of student-teacher collaboration in both research and curricular development or revision, teacher-to-teacher collaborative efforts, and collaborative approaches to academic administration (Romer, 1985). The CUE network mounts presentations and workshops at national higher education conferences, acts as a clearinghouse for information about collaborative work, publishes a newsletter, and works on publications. Additionally, the FIPSE-funded Collaborative Learning Resource Center at Lesley College in Cambridge, Massachusetts, is another clearinghouse, bringing together scholars, practitioners, and educational researchers interested in collaboration.

Collaborative Learning and Epistemological Theory

Those who structure their classrooms around collaboration can find philosophical confirmation of their approaches in recent scholarship in social constructionism and in feminist theory and pedagogy. Social constructionism, an expanding web of epistemological perspectives in several disciplines, springs from the assumption that knowledge is socially, rather than individually, constructed by communities of individuals. Knowledge is shaped, over time, by successive conversations, and by ever-changing social and political environments. The knowledge business should not be just the territory of competing scholars or experts, the social constructionists argue; the shaping and testing of ideas is something in which anyone can participate.

Theorists in the moral and intellectual development of women and in feminist pedagogy generally agree with the social constructionist view of knowledge creation and change. They believe that students cannot be regarded as a uniform body of isolated individuals poised to receive knowledge through uniform modes of information delivery. Rather, learners are diverse individuals whose understanding of reality is shaped by their gender, race, class, age, and cultural experience. Therefore, teaching is woefully inadequate if it is construed as an enterprise of "transmission" or "coverage." And learning is woefully limited if it is thought of as simply an exercise in "receiving" and "reflecting." To enable learners to move beyond superficial or merely procedural understanding of a subject, the teacher must invite them into a process of working out their own understandings and syntheses of the material, and developing their individual points of view toward it (Belenky, Clinchy, Goldberger, and Tarule, 1986).

Designing for Collaborative Learning

The glimpses of collaborative learning that opened this chapter suggest a broad range of formats and contexts in which these approaches flourish.

During a lecture, students might be asked to turn to a neighbor to formulate responses, raise questions, or solve problems. Students might work in teams to conduct and write up a laboratory report, field study, or longer research project. Groups of students might meet regularly to prepare homework or critique each other's writing, hold seminar discussions, or prepare for a presentation. What is essential is positive interdependence between students, a product to which everyone contributes, and a sense of commitment and responsibility to the group's preparation, process, and product.

For the faculty member, designing collaborative learning experiences requires careful thought about what active learning might entail in one's course or discipline. Meaningful, lasting learning requires students to use what is known to them, and what is becoming known. This involves linking the gathering aspects of learning to doing, constructing, and creating. Gathering means the "taking in" part of learning: taking in new information or ideas, by reading, watching, or listening. Doing is the "using" part: using what is gathered either to construct one's own understanding of the material or to create something new, for example, a poem, a sculpture, or a response. Too often, college classrooms have made learning largely a gathering process, and have relegated the doing/constructing/creating portions to occasional performances on quizzes or tests.

Sketching in the Possibilities. The first task for the teacher who is planning collaborative work for students is to examine the scope of a whole course and sketch the collaborative possibilities. Where and in how much of the course is collaboration appropriate? How can the gathering and the doing elements of the course be interwoven so that each element reinforces the other?

Developing the Collaborative Task. Framing the actual tasks or problems for collaborative work requires thinking through the particular kind of intellectual experiences or thinking tasks that students might undertake together. Most teachers realize that unstructured, freewheeling explorations do not sufficiently focus student energy, or challenge students to use what they know. Students are most stimulated when confronted with absorbing or puzzling tasks or questions and a clear sense of the product that is expected of them: for example, a synthesis, a conceptual framework, a comparison, an argument, an array of personal responses, or a dramatization.

With experience, faculty members find that they get better and better at preparing students for collaborative work, that is, at providing them with a common framework or background from which to begin, questions or problems that stimulate and stretch them, and a clear sense of expected outcomes of the group work. It takes some practice, and repeated observation of students grappling with ideas, to find those points of access, or "zones of proximal development" as Vygotsky called them, where students are challenged to move from what they know into the realm of what they do not quite yet know.

Thinking Through How Evaluation Will Work. A third design arena concerns feedback and accountability, critical elements in any collaborative enterprise. Several important issues should be addressed by faculty and students alike before the group work gets under way. If multiple small groups are working on problems or exploring issues simultaneously in a classroom, what will be the process for sharing or giving feedback on the results of work? When and how might the faculty member provide clarification, evaluation, or extension of the work that has been accomplished? Will the students have an opportunity to evaluate the nature of their own work, as well as their effort as an interdependent group? In what manner will they give the teacher feedback on the quality of the experience? How will the teacher carry out individual student evaluation when students are spending significant time working in teams?

Practice: The Best Teacher. There are several resources on managing collaborative learning, but the richest guides for collaborative teachers are their own experiments with teaching, the advice and experience of colleagues, and, most importantly, formal and informal feedback from the students themselves. Indeed, the collaborative classroom, brimming with data about the content and quality of student learning, is an ongoing lab for classroom research. The public learning taking place provides immediate feedback for the discerning teacher to use in improving collaborative designs. For faculty who offer the same courses year after year, the use of group work is a sure hedge against staleness. Each refinement of a collaborative learning design, and each new class's experience with it, recreates the material in fresh and provocative ways.

Reframing the Student Role

A class with high expectations about participation and collaboration requires substantial role shifts for students. It is not unusual to encounter student resistance to group work. Embedded in student expectations about classroom culture, and in the inertia of their own ingrained habits, such resistance is real and should be taken seriously.

As they move into collaborative learning settings, students find themselves grappling with shifts such as the following: (1) from listener, observer, and note taker to active problem solver, contributor, and discussant; (2) from low to moderate expectations of preparation for class to high expectations, frequently having to do with reading and preparing questions or other assigned work in advance; (3) from a private presence in the classroom to a public one; (4) from attendance dictated by personal choice to that having to do with community expectation; (5) from competition with peers to collaborative work with them; (6) from responsibilities and self-definition associated with learning independently to those associated with learning interdependently; and (7) from seeing teachers and texts as the sole sources of authority and knowledge to seeing peers, oneself, and the thinking of the community as additional and important sources of authority and knowledge.

These shifts are especially problematic for younger college learners. To them, the adjective "cooperative" has unfortunate residual connotations from high school. With reference to authorities, being cooperative has to do with obedience; with reference to peers, it usually means cheating. The idea of cooperation as helping and sharing for positive goals is often a completely foreign notion. Many students also have difficulty accepting that collaborative learning with peers is real learning and has value, so conditioned are they to expecting teachers to be the sole source of knowledge in the classroom.

Moreover, there are the risks inherent in the public nature of collaborative work. Such work almost always entails talk, and a great deal of it. Learning collaboratively, students are working out loud, and the learning is "live"—on the air, as it were, bloopers and all.

The faculty member, then, needs to set the context for collaborative work so that students can understand and reflect on its rationale, value, and immediate goals. Many teachers feel it is essential to engage students in discussion about the risks and responsibilities of working in groups, the challenges and opportunities inherent in learning from diverse perspectives, and the interplay between individualism and community. With the students, many faculty members develop a set of group norms or ground rules for coming to class prepared, working together responsibly, and resolving differences. They also work to create a safe environment for risk taking, where students' offerings, even the most tentative ones, are listened to attentively, and where disagreements are aired with respect. Many teachers make a practice of giving public value to the group process as well as to the thinking tasks, by asking each collaborative student team to evaluate not only the quality of its intellectual work but also the quality of its team work. With time, patience, and understanding, students usually break through their cautiousness, fear, and skepticism about collaboration and discover the stimulation and power of working in concert with others.

Reframing the Teacher Role

Whether novice or veteran in the collaborative learning process, faculty members engaged in this work have their own reframing to do, with regard to coverage, classroom roles, evaluation, and a variety of other issues. Particularly challenging is the process of reconciling one's sense of responsibility about course coverage with one's commitment to enabling students to learn on their own. Too often, faculty members think of course coverage in zero-sum terms, neglecting to ask whether students are really comprehending and integrating all that is being covered. Teachers who build their courses around group work do not belittle or abandon coverage or skills; indeed, they and their students are seriously and directly confronting matters of understanding and comprehension all the time. But the burden of "covering" (and of explicating and relating) has shifted from the teacher alone to the teacher and students together.

If this shift of responsibility helps to "dissolve the Atlas complex" (Finkel and Monk, 1983), wherein the teacher feels endlessly responsible for the class's entire intellectual agenda, it also poses interesting questions. Authority and expertise, power and control—highly intertwined matters for any teacher—all come up for examination and redefinition in the collaborative classroom. As students together begin assuming more responsibility for their learning, and as classroom time is directed more to conversational inquiry, teachers begin to sense subtle but powerful shifts in their role. As students begin to take up their part in the learning enterprise, teachers begin to see that they are not so much relinquishing control as they are sharing it in new ways. They discover that the lines of authority are not so much blurred as they are reshaped.

For example, collaborating teachers want to share their expertise without eclipsing students' beginning attempts to develop their own. They may not be playing the center-stage expert role continuously, but they must then choose what alternate roles to play, and when it would be most productive to play which role. They might be active co-learners, who work with students as the more expert peers in a process of mutual inquiry. They might use their expertise as workshop architects or simulation designers, who present students with questions or problems; they then remove themselves from the process, allowing the students to explore on their own while they watch from the sidelines and give expert feedback only at the end. Or they might choose a role in between, where they are the stimulators of student group work, who move from group to group observing and entering occasionally into the picture as friendly kibitzers.

Teachers also must consider the issue of authority relative to grading and evaluation within the collaborative context. By observing student work in interactive settings, faculty discover how well they have come to know their students, and how much data they have acquired for evaluating them. Because this information is at once so much more rich and diverse than what would normally emerge from occasional discussions, papers, or exams, it makes the grading process both more interesting and more complex. What remains problematic, however, is that faculty members are still the expert witnesses of student learning, and the holders of power relative to the grading process. And, more than any other factor, instructors' evaluative processes act to divide students, and to press the classroom atmosphere back into a competitive mode. Teachers need to clarify, for themselves as well as for students, their assumptions and expectations about evaluation as it relates to the collaborative work in the class, and about what evaluative weight will be given to team work and to individual work throughout the course. Teachers find it crucial to build an understanding of the evaluation process at the outset, and to remain vigilant about students' perceptions of evaluation throughout the course. Many teachers build evaluation responsibilities and skills in their students by involving them in self-evaluation as well as in peer and faculty evaluation.

Collaborative Learning and the Future

Faculty involved with collaborative learning remain deeply committed to it, in spite of its challenges. Many of these teachers are inspired by larger social imperatives, such as the needs for greater multicultural understanding and a more participatory democracy. But many more teachers are simply excited about what collaborative learning helps them discover in their students and in themselves. They relish the ways students emerge as confident, competent learners, who in turn stimulate them to reexamine their own work and thinking. They value each class they teach as a unique community, enriched by the subject matter but enriching it as well. Preliminary efforts to evaluate collaborative learning are encouraging: these kinds of approaches have been found to have a positive impact on student retention, achievement, and intellectual development, as well as on attitudinal and affective change, particularly in the areas of self-esteem and sensitivity to racial, ethnic, and gender differences (Cooper and Mueck, in press; MacGregor, 1987).

What then, does the future hold for collaborative learning? Are the collaborative learning vines healthy? While recent evidence indicates a remarkable growth surge, the ground for collaborative learning is not entirely fertile. The prevailing structures of most colleges simply do not foster effective group work. Fifty-minute hours, large class sizes, and fixed seating arrangements are only a few of the structures that still assume a "transmission" model of college teaching and learning. Reward systems for college teachers do not yet give high priority to pedagogical excellence; even where they do, there is little recognition of teaching innovation or experimentation, and few opportunities for teachers to collaborate on different approaches. Stereotypes of what collaborative learning is or entails may deter many potentially interested teachers from ever trying it out. Others who do try collaborative approaches without adequate support or preparation may feel less than successful and turn away with a sense of discomfort or failure. But what can hold back collaborative learning the most is our cultural biases toward competition and individualism, also strong vines in the American arbor that have a particularly tenacious presence in our academic institutions. The task of the collaborative learning effort, then, is not only to share and document effective models of collaborative teaching and learning but also to articulate its role and value in American education and society.

While there are barriers to the spread of collaborative learning, other trends, both inside and outside the academy, propel the work forward. Collaborative learning networks, and learning community and other curricular efforts, are expanding. Many of these endeavors find reinforcement in major studies and reports on effective teaching and learning (Chickering and Gamson, 1987; National Institute of Education, 1984), and on student success in college (Tinto, 1987). While experience and sophistication develop on the practice side, there is growing commitment to collaboration from the general education sector. Social interaction skills, appreciation of racial, gender, and ethnic differences, and civic awareness and responsibility are emerging as essential outcomes of academic experiences, not simply of student life activities.

These developments are modest, however, compared to the rapidly growing emphases on social interdependence and collaboration both in the workplace and in public arenas. Horizontal and participatory forms of management have taken their places alongside more traditional vertical and authoritarian approaches in political contexts, and public involvement and partnership-building efforts are burgeoning worldwide. The arena of conflict resolution, once equated almost entirely with adversarial processes, has begun to include new, more collaborative forms of negotiated and mediated settlement processes. In what is becoming a daunting landscape of social and environmental predicaments, these new forms of management and problem solving represent small, promising sparks of constructive change. Workplaces, the nation, and the world will increasingly call for more responsible and responsive community builders and problem solvers, and all our educational systems will have to search for ways to meet this demand. All these trends may combine to create a much more favorable climate for the growth of collaborative learning approaches into the twenty-first century.

Shared Inquiry as a Process of Reform

As it becomes more widely practiced, collaborative learning has profound implications. It could change the nature of conventional undergraduate classrooms, and it could help to develop a much more civically active populace. Yet, the collaborative learning agenda is really about individual learners, and how it enables them to learn about learning and themselves. While there are larger educational and societal implications, collaborative learning can only begin and grow as a small-scale reform, the kind that springs within individuals, a few at a time. Collaboration in classroom settings can reveal that learning itself is always an occasion for reform. The process of shared inquiry invites students and teachers to develop the habit of seeing their knowledge as continuously evolving, indeed reforming, through dialogues with the self, others, and the world.

References

Belenky, M. F., Clinchy, B. M., Goldberger, N. R., and Tarule, J. M. *Women's Ways of Knowing*. New York: Basic Books, 1986.

Chickering, A. W., and Gamson, Z. "Seven Principles for Good Practice in Undergraduate Education." *American Association for Higher Education Bulletin*, 1987, *39*, 3-7.

Cooper, J., and Mueck, R. "Student Involvement in Learning: Cooperative Learning and College Instruction." *Journal of Excellence in College Teaching*, in press.

Finkel, D. L., and Monk, G. S. "Teachers and Learning Groups: Dissolving the Atlas Complex." In C. Bouton and R. Y. Garth (eds.), *Learning in Groups*. New Directions for Teaching and Learning, no. 14. San Francisco: Jossey-Bass, 1983.

Gabelnick, F., MacGregor, J., Matthews, R. S., and Smith, B. L. *Learning Communities: Creating Connections Among Students, Faculty, and Disciplines*. New Directions for Teaching and Learning, no. 41. San Francisco: Jossey-Bass, 1990.

Johnson, D. W., and others. "Effect of Cooperative, Competitive and Individualistic Goal Structures on Achievement: A Meta-Analysis." *Psychological Bulletin*, 1981, *89*, 47-62.

MacGregor, J. *Intellectual Development of Students in Learning Communities*. Washington Center Occasional Paper, no. 1. Olympia, Wash.: The Evergreen State College, 1987.

National Institute for Education. *Involvement in Learning: Realizing the Potential for Higher Education*. Final Report of the Study Group of the Conditions of Excellence in Higher Education. Washington, D.C.: National Institute for Education, 1984.

Romer, K. T. (ed.). *CUE: Models of Collaboration in Undergraduate Education*. Providence, R.I.: Brown University Press, 1985.

Slavin, R. E. "When Does Cooperative Learning Increase Student Achievement?" *Psychological Bulletin*, 1983, *94*, 429-445.

Tinto, V. *Leaving College: Rethinking the Causes and Cures of Student Attrition*. Chicago: University of Chicago Press, 1987.

Jean MacGregor is associate director of The Washington Center for Improving the Quality of Undergraduate Education at The Evergreen State College, Olympia, Washington.

*The Writing Across the Curriculum movement has been
encouraging instructors in a wide range of disciplines to
consider writing as a tool for learning. This chapter discusses
why writing can be such a powerful tool, but also why the
movement is having problems in implementation.*

Writing to Learn:
Back to Another Basic

Sandra Tomlinson

In a documentary film made just before he died, Robert Frost (1963b)
reminisced about his time as a college teacher. He said that he liked to
"do something" to a class, "not tell them something, but do something
to them." "One of my favorite ways," he said, "was to scare them about
what it was to have what I really call an idea. To say what Ring Lardner
calls a bucketful. To say something that *is* something." With obvious
distaste Frost complained that students write "perfunctory papers that
don't have anything in them, not one crack to the carload." He blamed
this lack of substance not on the students but on their teachers: "Some
people think that if they pile up enough knowledge, it's like piling up
oily rags in the basement, that they'll burst into flame of themselves—
light the world up. They say to you in school, you know, 'Here, we're
going to dump a lot of material on you now. We'll back up this load to
you.' And then they say, 'Now it's coming. Assimilate it.' And you die
under it. . . . The accumulators."

In his remarks Frost articulated a widespread and familiar problem.
Teachers agonize over the ability and superficiality of student thinking.
When surveyed, faculty have listed "immature or undeveloped thinking
habits" as the most serious deficiency in student responses (Fulwiler and
Jones, 1979, p. 308). Yet, many of us continue to pile up knowledge, to
give out megabytes of information, expecting our students to gain enlightenment through accumulation. To be sure, it is not irresponsibility that
causes us to pursue this approach to teaching. The information explosion
has increased our feelings of urgency that there is too much to cover in
our limited semesters and quarters. We feel that we do not have sufficient

time to linger over points. And we hear voices like that of E. D. Hirsch, Jr. (1987) reminding us of the decline in our students' command of the shared knowledge needed for even basic reading literacy. But, in the face of conflicting needs, we must reexamine what it means to "cover" material. We cannot assume that because we have lectured on a given topic in class, our students have learned the material; dispensing information is not the same as assuring understanding.

Writing to Think

We, of course, hope that our students will figure out how to think about and use the information we give them. We want them to learn to act like professionals. We want them to think both critically and imaginatively. We love the intelligent insights, the bursts of creative fire, and the clear explanations, dense with appropriate support. But having what Frost "really calls an idea" does not happen just by assimilation of material. Saying something "that *is* something" requires going beyond memorization. It requires analysis and synthesis, and the whole spectrum of skills described in Bloom's (1984) taxonomy. The kind of learning we want to witness and bear witness to demands complex, closely interwoven thought processes. In any discipline, these skills can be developed and enhanced through writing. In fact, learning to think in the way Frost meant *requires* writing, for writing is the only way most people can hold information long enough to transform it into original, substantive ideas.

Writing to Learn

It may be fairly obvious that writing is a necessary means to higher-order thinking. But, even at the simplest level of knowledge acquisition, writing is an aid. All learning is on some level active learning. In order to acquire knowledge that we can actually understand and use, we must take what we already know and add it to what we are trying to know (Weinstein, 1985, p. 5). To make sense of new information, we have to relate it to prior knowledge and experience. Most often we make sense of it through some process of elaboration—paraphrase, summary, comparison, application, and questioning, for example. Without writing, all of the elaboration schemes will quickly overload our memories. With writing we can retain the information long enough to work with it and to store it in long-term memory. Writing is helpful even if we do not expect students to go beyond knowledge acquisition. However, if we expect critical or creative thinking, it is essential.

The Writing Across the Curriculum Movement

Participating in a movement James Britton (1975) called Writing Across the Curriculum, many teachers have recognized that only through writing can students develop and use the higher-order thinking skills Frost was talking about. Janet Emig (1977) argues convincingly that writing offers a unique means of combining all of the attributes of hand, eye, and brain needed for learning. Professors in diverse fields have eloquently testified to the effectiveness of writing as a tool of learning. History professor Gerald Belcher (1979), for example, claims, "no matter how much content students are given, it is stillborn if they cannot make sense of it, order it, use, and finally, express it." Mathematics instructor William Geeslin (1977, p. 115) has students write out explanations of mathematical concepts given that writing "appears to improve students' learning and performance on traditional tasks." In a defense of writing in all disciplines, Lois Barry (1984, p. 10) says, "Writing is one of the most powerful teaching tools we have. . . . There is no dispute about the power of writing to help students learn and to give them an invaluable tool in shaping what they know." Finally, one of the leaders of the Writing Across the Curriculum movement, Toby Fulwiler (1980, p. 16), attests the great benefit of writing in any classroom: "Every time students write, they individualize instruction; the act of silent writing, even for five minutes, generates ideas, observations, emotions. Regular writing makes it harder for students to remain passive."

So Why Is the Movement Floundering?

Testimonies, however, do not tell the whole story. In almost every college and university, one can find some instructors who use writing to help students learn, but relatively few colleges have made it a requirement (Russell, 1987). Writing as a mode of learning seems to remain on the fringes of academe, found mainly in journal articles, in professional development workshops, and in the classes of particularly experimental or conscientious teachers. For awhile the movement seemed to catch hold. History teachers put term paper assignments back into their classes, only to find the papers still perfunctory and the grading still tedious. It has become fairly obvious that traditional kinds of writing assignments, however frequent, do not necessarily improve either knowledge acquisition or thinking skills. The lengthy term paper, full of undigested and undistilled information, seldom produces critical or creative thinking, or, for that matter, long-term information retention. Neither do we always get the mature thinking we want from the long essay question in which the student is asked to "discuss the causes of the Civil War." Such a topic usually requires little more than memorization skills, even when it is presented as a thought-provoking prompt. A multiple choice or true-false test can accomplish as much and will be easier to grade. It is also unlikely that the long, one-shot assignments in which the students turn in their writing after a certain number of weeks without any feedback in the process can produce that desirable "crack to the carload" or Ring Lardner's "bucketful."

Perhaps, once again, we need to reexamine our philosophy and our methods. Despite our longing to see fresh, creative, thoughtful work, we have continued to insist on information recall. But the purpose in writing as a way to learn is not to repeat what the teacher says, or to give the right answer to something, or to copy the opinions of experts. Its purpose is to move us toward a greater understanding of whatever we are examining: a math problem or a work of literature. As a learning mode, writing is a process of discovery; without the discovery it is pointless. Donald Murray (1989) tells student writers to expect surprise and to not be satisfied until the surprise comes. One of the greatest of life's joys is what Frost (1963a) called the "surprise of remembering something I didn't know I knew." When students experience this joy, they have begun to think. Traditional writing assignments too often omit the discovery and the surprise. It is interesting that in so doing, they may also omit the real acquisition of information. For according to information theory, the amount of information in any communication is proportional to the amount of surprise it produces in the receiver.

How to Save the Movement

In order to make Writing Across the Curriculum work effectively, we have to be just as creative and critical in our teaching methods as we expect our students to be in their learning. The use of writing as a way to learn is not necessarily quick and simple. Requiring daily or frequent writing is not an easier way to teach. It demands a closer contact with students' work in progress than we may be accustomed to providing. For if we expect writing to help our students learn, we need to read or listen to their writing and give them immediate feedback as often as we can. We cannot just make an assignment and walk out of the room and expect the writing to create miracles by itself. Finally, we have to be willing to allow students the clumsy phrase and the misspelled word, for if we look at every piece of writing as a product to be graded by the standards of publication, we cannot expect our students to write without fear.

Even as we begin to think of specific writing tasks for our students, we must move away from our traditional attitudes. We cannot progress by simply putting old wine in new bottles. We may need to be a little more trusting in the capabilities of our students to think productively about even new material. They can offer a freshness that will give us some new perspectives on our disciplines. We need to let the students discover more things for themselves. And we must definitely be open to a variety of assignments. In part, our job as teachers is to create an atmosphere of experimentation and thoughtfulness that will engage students' imaginations and intelligence so that they can turn new knowledge into what Frost "really calls an idea."

Helpful Principles

There are several principles to designing writing assignments that foster learning:

    1. Assignments have to be at least stimulating enough to kindle expectation. Students are not necessarily as interested in our disciplines as we are, so we often need the clever catch or the controversial issue to capture their attention. For example, in an ethics class, make it a point to have them deal with issues such as abortion or human rights. In history ask students to write about the effects of slavery on modern attitudes toward race and color, or about the relationship between Nazism and slavery.

    2. Writing needs to be frequent enough to maintain involvement throughout a course. Have students write at least a little every day. The practice helps, and it can become a habit.

    3. Writing assignments should be a means of comprehension monitoring whereby students can check their own understanding. They can summarize material they have read or lectures you have given, write out questions they have about the material, outline chapters, or paraphrase paragraphs.

    4. It helps if students can apply information in some familiar context. Jaime Escalante (1989) has claimed, for example, that he spends a tremendous amount of time trying to find ways to explain mathematical concepts by pointing out their relationships to things familiar and important to his students, for example, figuring the angle of the basketball's entry into the basket as an application of a calculus principle. Unless students can actually relate new information to something they already know, they will have difficulty retaining it.

    5. Finally, professors should make sure that students share their writing with others. In *The Journal Book*, Toby Fulwiler (1987, p. 7), for example, suggests that "every time you ask students to write in class, do something active and deliberate with what they have written: have volunteers read whole entries; have everyone read one sentence to the whole class; have neighbors share one passage with each other, etc."

    Directed journal writing is an excellent way to fulfill all of these principles. It can replace daily quizzes by requiring students to respond to and ask questions about their reading assignments or class lectures. Journal writing can become a daily expectation. Also, because they do not have to be graded in an analytic or traditional way, journals serve as places where students can take risks. Through journal assignments, we can encourage many different kinds of thinking: We can ask students to summarize material, formulate questions about discussions or reading assignments, relate new information to their personal lives, apply the principles of a discipline to actual cases, or explain the process by which they have arrived at a solution to a problem. In journals they can analyze, synthesize, summarize, apply, or create. In addition, journals can give students a constant means of checking their comprehension of a subject. Through daily, informal writing about new material, students can keep in touch with what they understand or do not understand. If students are asked to share their journal writing with the rest of the class, or with partners in a group, journals can also serve as excellent prompts to class discussion and as methods of peer teaching. Daily journal writing to ponder over, read aloud, or talk about keeps students actively involved in and responsible for their own learning.

So too, of all the modes of writing to learn, the case approach, in which students apply ideas or principles to actual or hypothetical situations, is one of the most productive, and it certainly allows for great variation. William J. McCleary (1985, p. 208) advocates the case approach because it "contributes to the learning of . . . concepts" by requiring "active use of the concepts." Assignments can be both inventive and thought provoking. Philosophy students, for example, could be asked to have Aristotle, Kant, Sartre, and Mill debate the ethics of euthanasia in a dialogue entitled "Whose Life Is This Anyway?" Such an application requires that students come to grips with the principles of Aristotle's *Nicomachian Ethics,* Kant's categorical imperative, Sartre's existentialism, and Mill's utilitarianism. In a particularly inventive essay, Meredith Michaels (1989, p. 391) asks students to argue which set of parents should pay tuition when one college student's brain is transplanted into another college student's body. A short paper focusing on this problem can lead students to intense thinking about the questions of personal identity raised by great philosophers such as Hume and Locke. The case approach works in courses as wide-ranging as auto mechanics and metaphysics, for effective use of the case requires students to understand principles, definitions, competing theories, and methods well enough to apply them to actual or true-to-life situations. In other words, the case study requires that they act like professionals in their fields.

Avoiding the "Overworked Professor" Syndrome

Fears that keep professors from assigning writing are not always valid. Not all student writing must be carefully read or graded. Facing a lecture class of five hundred students, an instructor obviously cannot read all of the students' daily writing, but he or she can count pages, look for word clues to suggest that a student is on the subject, do spot checks in class while the students are writing, use writing to spark class discussion, or ask students to share their writing with each other. Professors can also assign group papers that actually imitate the kind of collaborative writing that often occurs in professional settings. Also, writing assignments can be quite brief. When asked to write exactly twenty-five words summarizing an article, defining a term, or offering a "recipe" for a solution to a problem that has principles or terms as ingredients, a student is forced to have a more exact understanding of the material and to articulate it with greater precision or care than if the teacher had called for a longer paper. Nor should professors worry that they are expected to become English teachers. Their job is not to grade the grammar, spelling, or punctuation. When writing to learn is the intent of an assignment, writing is a means to understanding, not just an end product.

Implications for the Future

If the Writing Across the Curriculum movement does spread across the nation to become "woven so tightly into the fabric of the institution as to resist the subtle unraveling effect of academic politics" (Russell, 1987, p. 191), teaching and learning will necessarily go in new directions. Writing to learn requires students to take charge of their own education. It requires teachers to become helpmates and facilitators rather than dispensers of knowledge who, to return to Frost, "back up this load" and "dump a lot of material on you." Students who are accustomed to walking into a class and turning on their cassette recorders will find their expectations uncomfortably shifted. And students who complain that they do not see the relevance of abstract theories to their future jobs will, we hope, find themselves applying those theories more like professionals. Writing assignments that require frequent applications of principles should better prepare students for the work force. And even though it is sometimes easier for students to remain passive and for the teacher to adopt the role of informer and expert, if the Writing Across the Curriculum movement grows, there will be an increasing awareness on both sides of the desk that the best process of learning is a dialogue. In the past, teachers have too often acted like critics, sitting high on their pedestals, far away from the process, pronouncing "thumbs up" or "thumbs down." As instructors begin to act like tutors, Socratic gadflies probing and prodding students to think and learn, students can begin to experience the joy of discovery that Frost talked about. Putting old and new information together to form a new idea is a kind of epiphany. Even the most passive student cannot resist the pleasure of discovery once it comes.

In many respects, then, writing to learn is just another part of the teaching effectiveness trend toward student-centered instruction. It is also, in a way, one facet of the back-to-basics movement. Writing has always been one of the three R's. But we left behind its power when we exiled it to the English classroom. We forgot that it is basic because it is perhaps the best single activity to generate and organize thought. Returning to writing will mean discarding our supermarket theories of education. Students are not consumers coming to buy knowledge, or, if they are or we have allowed them to think that they are, then we are mistaken about what we are doing. Professors are not acting more responsibly when they monopolize every minute of class. Students will not learn less when they have to spend more time writing. To develop critical and creative thinking skills, they have to wrestle with the questions raised by the material, find the relevance of the material to their lives and disciplines, enter into dialogues and debates about truth and viability, and engage in perpetual problem-solving. The oily rags we have piled up in the basement will burst into flames only if sparked by minds actively engaged in higher-order thinking. When used as a way to learn, writing can kindle that spark.

References

Barry, L. *The Busy Professor's Travel Guide to Writing Across the Curriculum.* La Grande, Oreg.: Eastern Oregon State College, 1984.

Belcher, G. Paper presented at the Conference on College Composition and Communication. Minneapolis, Minn., April 6, 1979.

Bloom, B. (ed.). *Taxonomy of Educational Objectives: The Classification of Educational Goals. Handbook.* Vol. 1: *Cognitive Domain.* New York: Longman, 1984.

Britton, J. *The Development of Writing Abilities.* London: Macmillan, 1975.

Emig, J. "Writing as a Mode of Learning." *College Composition and Communication,* 1977, *28,* 122–128.

Escalante, J. "Stand and Deliver: Helping Students to Succeed Against the Odds." Address to the American Association of Higher Education, Chicago, April 1989.

Frost, R. "The Figure a Poem Makes." In R. Graves (ed.), *Selected Poems of Robert Frost.* New York: Holt, Rinehart & Winston, 1963a.

Frost, R. *A Lover's Quarrel with the World.* A film by R. Hughes and C. Zwerin. Boston: WGBH Education Foundation, 1963b.

Fulwiler, T. "Journals Across the Disciplines." *English Journal,* 1980, *69* (12), 14–19.

Fulwiler, T. *The Journal Book.* Upper Montclair, N.J.: Boynton/Cook, 1987.

Fulwiler, T., and Jones, R. "Writing in Biology: A Seminar." *College Composition and Communication,* 1979, *30,* 308–310.

Geeslin, W. "Using Writing About Mathematics as a Teaching Technique." *Mathematics Teacher,* 1977, *70,* 112–115.

Hirsch, E. D. *Cultural Literacy: What Every American Needs to Know.* Boston: Houghton Mifflin, 1987.

McCleary, W. J. "A Case Approach for Teaching Academic Writing." *College Composition and Communication,* 1985, *36,* 203–212.

Michaels, M. "Personal Identity." In R. C. Solomon (ed.), *Introducing Philosophy: A Text with Integrated Readings*. (4th ed.) New York: Harcourt Brace Jovanovich, 1989.

Murray, D. M. *Expecting the Unexpected: Teaching Myself—and Others—to Read and Write*. Upper Montclair, N.J.: Boynton/Cook, 1989.

Russell, D. R. "Writing Across the Curriculum and the Communications Movement: Some Lessons from the Past." *College Composition and Communication*, 1987, *38*, 184–193.

Weinstein, C. E. "Assessment and Training of Student Learning Strategies." In R. R. Schmeck (ed.), *Learning Styles and Learning Strategies*. New York: Plenum, 1985.

Sandra Tomlinson is assistant dean of Humanities and associate professor of English at Galveston College, Galveston, Texas.

*Case discussion is less like marching an orderly band of hikers
on a predetermined course across the terrain than it is like
bringing a scattered group of parachutists into contact from
all the random places they have landed.*

Teaching with Cases:
Learning to Question

John Boehrer, Marty Linsky

> One encounters not a problem but a difficulty, and the
> hardest part of the task is in recasting the difficulty as the
> kind of problem that one knows how to solve. We do not
> encounter problems, but situations in which we need to
> discover what the problem is.
> —Bouton and Garth (1983, p. 79)

In a diverse educational setting, a variety of learning groups working in
separate fields of study and at different levels of experience can be found
pursuing skill and knowledge through a common process. What follow
are just a few of many possible illustrations of the case method, an active
learning approach that has both ancient roots and contemporary variations. It is a teaching strategy defined both by its characteristic texts and
by its ways of employing them: (1) undergraduates taking an introduction
to public policy at a midwestern university wade into the intricacies of
government decision making by navigating the course of action taken to
head off the feared swine flu epidemic of the mid 1970s; (2) in a night
class at a community college, management students act out a series of
role-plays to explore the dynamics involved when a new administrator
runs into resistance from the nurses in a hospital where she is attempting
to increase accountability; (3) in an amphitheater classroom at an eastern
graduate school, master's degree students tackle the problem of placing
an economic value on the seemingly intangible environmental benefits at
issue in deciding whether to dam the scenic Tuolumne River to provide

power and water for San Francisco; (4) teaching colleagues on a small college faculty struggle with uncertainty about the place of personal values in the classroom as they experience the dilemma of a teacher confronted by the apparent racism of a student who refuses to work with another; (5) seasoned reporters, attending a seminar at a journalism think tank in Florida, argue about what to do when a colleague breaches an accepted standard of professional ethics; and (6) meeting in a special White House seminar, senior political appointees of a new administration project themselves into the situation of William Ruckelshaus as he faces the challenge of generating both internal commitment to and external support for the newly created Environmental Protection Agency.

The activity common to these separate scenes is case discussion: interactive, student-centered exploration of realistic and specific narratives that provide grist for inductive learning. The students are engaged in the intellectual, and emotional, exercise of facing complex problems and making critical decisions without the constraints imposed by reality, for example, limited time and information and pervasive uncertainty. Considering the situations from the protagonist's perspective, which calls on analysis to inform action, the students strive to resolve questions that have no single right answer. Their differing views and approaches produce a creative tension that fuels the enterprise and a synergistic outcome that both recognizes and exceeds their individual contributions. In their efforts to find solutions and reach decisions through discussion, they sort out factual data, apply analytic tools, articulate issues, reflect on their relevant experience, and draw conclusions they can carry forward to new situations. In the process, they acquire substantive knowledge, develop analytic and collaborative skills, and gain in self-confidence and attention to detail.

A case discussion differs in some important respects from what is conventional in many college and university classrooms. The students engage in the text rather than examine it. They are active and animated: offering ideas, raising questions, building on each other's statements, constructing a collective analysis, reframing the discussion, challenging the teacher, and learning with and from each other as much or more than from the teacher. The teacher is also active, and frequently mobile: initiating discussion and drawing the class into it, inviting engagement in the issues, amplifying some students' comments and summarizing others', writing *their* words on the board, relating separate remarks and pointing up opposing views, feeding the group's thinking back to it, and pulling the threads of conversation together and tying them to the course's themes; in short, the teacher is structuring and facilitating the students' work rather than delivering information, giving explanations, or providing answers. The emphasis is on the students' reasoning and expression, on their capacity to structure the problem and work out a solution. It is also on the process as well as the substance of inquiry, and a case discussion often ends with questions as well as conclusions.

What is going on here challenges what Cantor (1953) calls the "assumptions of orthodox teaching," for example, that subject matter is the same to the learner and the teacher, and that the teacher is responsible for it being learned; that knowledge is more important than learning; and that education is primarily an intellectual process. Case teaching invokes the "propositions of modern learning," for example, that learning depends on wanting to learn, and not knowing the answers; that every student learns in a unique way what he or she is interested in learning, and learns best when allowed to respond freely to a situation; and that learning is also an emotional experience.

Though it is unconventional in many current settings, there is nothing new about the case method. It is as old as learning from experience, and, in fact, it is a strategy for bringing that mode of learning into the classroom, teaching it as a practice, and accelerating it by providing more frequent and varied problems than life usually offers in equal time. The strategy derives from the observation that accomplished practitioners in any field have built their capacity to face new challenges with skills and confidence by working through many previous problems. As long as there have been mentors and guides who have educated students by leading them through thoughtful consideration of actual problems, there has, in fact, been case teaching. Perhaps because it is really a very fundamental approach, rather than the exotic practice it is sometimes thought to be, it continues to find new applications in familiar fields, new educational purposes to serve, new subjects to illuminate, and new means of expression in modern technology.

In this chapter, after briefly reviewing the origins of the case method, we look at the question of what is a case, some ideas about learning implicit in case teaching, the range of purposes it can serve in the classroom, the basic ground rules for case discussion, including the critical role of questions, and, finally, some new directions that case teaching is taking.

Background

As a modern pedagogical practice, the case method has roots in legal and medical education as far back as the last century. In both those settings, actual cases have been used to illustrate and teach general principles as well as specific content and methods of analysis. These professions, like many other endeavors, also have a tradition of apprenticeship, learning through supervised practice. Case discussion can be understood as an abstraction of that process removed to the classroom. The basic approach to case discussion that underlies most current applications is usually attributed to the Harvard Business School (HBS), where it was pioneered during the first half of the century. Faculty there found that educating students by having them work through the problems posed by scores of cases developed their capacity to conduct sound analysis and take effective action to solve challenging management problems.

Since World War II, the case method has evolved into a highly inter-active discussion process that has proved capable of engaging a diverse range of students from school children to senior practitioners. It has come to serve subjects as disparate as microeconomics and the ministry, and to enlighten students on everything from the dilemmas of dating to the nuances of nuclear arms control. Developed to train future and pre-sent business executives, it now contributes to the education of profes-sionals in such fields as accounting, engineering, negotiation, nursing, and teaching itself. Recent applications have taken it into new fields, such as international relations, and coupled it with contemporary tech-nology. Traditionally limited to print, some cases now incorporate com-puter spreadsheets and interactive video to enhance presentation of the material and increase student engagement. These intriguing develop-ments extend the potential of the case method while preserving its essen-tial character and purpose.

What *Is* a Case?

The relation between the artifact of a case and its functional purpose is a crucial aspect of the case method. To grasp this, it is useful to think of a case in several ways: as a document or text, as a story, as a vehicle for discussion, and as an event.

The variety of forms that even the traditional printed case can take, from half-page vignettes to multipart documents replete with tables, graphs, and exhibits, indicates that format, though it affects utility, is hardly definitive. Indeed, we would argue that a group can find grist for case discussion in a play, a news clip, or an incident reported by one of the group members. Executive education programs, and shorter seminars with students who have considerable professional experience, sometimes draw cases from participants, who may present them orally in class or write them up in advance. Other media than the written and spoken word can accommodate cases, too. Films and videotapes can both enhance and supplant more traditional texts. And the sophisticated interactive computer and video simulations now emerging give new dimension to the text as well as to the learning process.

In the many forms it can take, a case is generically *a story;* it presents the concrete narrative detail of actual, or at least realistic, events. It has a plot, usually exposition and characters, sometimes even dialogue. In fact, cases are sometimes literally stories. Robert Coles (1989) teaches issues of practice to medical students with fiction; he has written compellingly about his experience using novels as vehicles for case discussion in his book *The Call of Stories.* In other contexts, the story lies inchoate in original documents, used singly or assembled. Cases in law recount first the facts, then the opinion. In the study of business or public management, cases are usually more deliberately crafted stories, selective presentations designed to focus on specific teaching points. Some are written with the elegance and skill of first-class literary productions, but they need not be to constitute effective teaching vehicles. For years, we have used the simple two-paragraph story of a dilemma facing a state senator on a key vote as the basis for a powerful and deep discussion of theories of representation and the conflicting obligations of a legislator in a democracy.

It is its utility as a *vehicle for* just such an *interaction* that comes closest to defining what a case really is, because it is the functioning of the case that is important, not the packaging. A good case is one that serves its intended purposes, including, centrally, a rich and lively discussion of the issues that the teacher wants the students to confront. A variety of factors contribute to a case's capacity to do that. Of course, the quality of the discussion also depends on the leader and the class. The best case is of little value in the hands of an unskilled teacher or unwilling students.

Bennett and Chakravarthy (1978) surveyed faculty and students at HBS to discover what engages students in a case. The main features they identified aptly characterize cases outside the bounds of business management. Besides telling a story, they concluded, a good case presents an *interest-provoking issue* and promotes *empathy with the central characters.* It delineates their individual perspectives and personal circumstances well enough to enable students to understand the characters' experience of the issue. The importance of the compelling issue and the empathetic character reflects the fact that cases typically focus on the intersection between organizational or situational dynamics and individual perception, judgment, and action (Towl, 1969).

Another dimension of cases that affects their utility is *length.* Like the findings of the HBS study, our experience suggests that written cases longer than fifteen pages tend to lose their vitality as discussion vehicles in most settings, at least those that fall within the framework of a traditional hour to hour-and-a-half class. Longer and more complex cases may work better if extended over several classes. In one course, we use a short book (in essence, a long case) as the material for discussion in two consecutive classes early in the semester and then come back to it later in the term.

The HBS researchers also found that students tend to be engaged by the *demand for a decision.* So-called decision-forcing cases, which present the problem prospectively, can stimulate a lively process of generating, analyzing, and selecting options. They pose the classic question, "What would you do?" Often, they break the story into parts, presenting a succession of decision points. Typically, each part relates what became of the preceding uncertainty and leads up to a new question. Sometimes a sequel reveals what finally happened in the case, to satisfy curiosity and bring the story to a close, but not to provide an "answer." Retrospective cases, which tell the whole story, including the end, tend to foster more reflective discussions in which students work to interpret what happened in the case and derive lessons from it. Some of these cases also consist of parts, to enable students to focus on different phases of the story and encourage them to think predictively about the consequences of action.

The *credibility* of the narrative was not a variable in the HBS study; the cases considered there related actual events. There are also hypothetical cases, though, and opinions about them differ. (These are not the same as disguised cases, which are entirely real but fictionalized in such details as names and places to preserve the privacy of sources and their organizations.) Case method purists argue that the actuality of case events is crucial, that only a real case can make a legitimate, and therefore effective, claim on student identification with the situation and the people involved in it. We disagree.

It is true that actuality has a powerful impact on student willingness to struggle with issues in the concrete terms of a case. And a real story is an effective barrier to the often tempting student escape that either the situation is preposterous or that it results from the obvious folly of the protagonist. ("How did X, a reasonable person, allow this to happen?" is often a powerful question.) But we find that a great variety of materials, real and imaginative, can serve as vehicles for enabling students to project themselves into a concrete, practical situation and to engage in productive discussion of the issues. A hypothetical case may be vulnerable to student rejection for lack of realism, but a real story may fail to engage their empathy too. That is the issue: whether the students can connect with the story.

Finally, it is useful to consider that like a play, which is also a text, a story, and a vehicle for engaging thoughts and feelings, a case is ultimately an *event*. Each performance of a play is unique because the action is live and the audience is new. Each discussion of a case is even more singular: the students improvise the conversation and interpret the story according to their own experiences, perceptions, and judgments. The discussion is the fulfillment of the case's purpose; until that event occurs, the case, however simple or elaborate, is mere potential. We think it worthwhile to view a case as an event because doing so reminds us that what matters about a case is what any particular set of students makes of it, that what they bring to it and what they take away are what it is for them.

Ideas About Learning with Cases

At HBS the thinking was, and still is, that repeated classroom encounters with issues that managers actually face, expressed in the concrete detail of cases, will produce problem solvers and decision makers capable of taking effective action in new situations. The relatively unstructured, but often intense, interaction of case discussion will give them a head start on coping with the real world because it will demand the effort to deal with constraints like limited time and imperfect information and present the need to operate within the context of interpersonal relationships and organizational dynamics. The process will expand their capacity to learn from experience.

Certain ideas about learning are at work here that extend to broader applications of the case method. The most basic is that *learning is purposeful: it results from the pursuit of a goal.* Genuine, self-motivated learning accompanies the effort to achieve a personally desired outcome (Kraft, 1978). Addressing a real (or realistic) problem as if it were one's own, which is the core activity of case learning, invokes the natural process of acquiring knowledge and skill, not for their own sake but for their contribution to reaching an objective. The immediate, specific problem is central to case learning; contending with it drives the process. Because it comes about in this purposeful way, the knowledge that results tends to remain active and usable, distinct, in Whitehead's (1929) terms, from the inert, inaccessible knowledge often acquired through more traditional academic means.

An idea more specific to the case method itself is that *case discussion can approximate the professional environment,* for example, legal analysis, medical diagnosis, or managerial decision making. That is, the classroom can be a forum for the kind of discourse, and the associated learning, that characterize actual practice. It is not surprising that the case method has taken hold first and strongest in law schools, medical schools, and business schools, which are training students for professional careers. In this sense, it is connected to the tradition of apprenticeship. Case discussion gives each student the opportunity to work on his or her own professional issues, to practice the profession, as it were, in a protected environment under the supervision of a senior person. Much of the expansion in the use of cases comes from the realization that if the case method can educate students about ideas and behavior related to their professional lives, then it ought also to apply to ideas and behavior related to their private lives: as democratic citizens, as parents and spouses, as consumers of news, as members of a community, and as ethical human beings.

Another idea central to the case method is that *experience and learning unlock each other:* experience provides valid data for learning, and learning organizes experience. HBS case-teaching exponent Andrew Towl notes that "cases are catalysts to speed the process for learning from experience" (Erskine, Leenders, and Mauffette-Leenders, 1981, p. 10). Learning to learn from experience, to learn in the process of it, and to learn one's way through it are fundamental objectives of the case method. Brown, Collins, and Duguid (1989, p. 32) argue that "knowledge is situated, being in part a product of the activity, context, and culture in which it is developed and used." Case discussion treats knowledge as situated and trains students to draw it from, and use it in, their experience. In wrestling with the problem of a case, the students engage in a collective learning exercise in the attempt to master the immediate experience of the problem. At the same time, the process encourages them both to apply their personal experience to the problem and to reflect back on it in light of the discussion. In the end, it asks them to rely on their own experience of the discussion to determine the meaning, and therefore the lessons, of it. Case teaching has the inevitable by-product of validating student experience, by using that of others as grist for their learning and by making theirs so central to the process. This outcome makes a significant contribution to the goal of moving students toward autonomous, self-directed learning as the means of coping with new experience.

Finally, the case method incorporates the idea that *students can learn from one another,* in more than one sense. In the process of case discussion, individual students offer information and insight that then become available to the rest of the group. The most significant learning they do from one another, however, is really more subtle and even more profound than that. It results more from the interaction than from the information. In a good case discussion students learn by engaging with each other and with each other's ideas, by asserting something and then having it questioned, challenged, and thrown back to them so that they can reflect on what they hear and refine what they say. It is so important to recognize that this can be done more in a cooperative than in a competitive spirit. Students can build on as well as critique each other's statements. A general lesson they can draw from their participation is that they can advance the discussion without having to outsmart each other, that in the process of collective inquiry the product of the class as a whole improves and the learning of each member increases.

Why Use Cases? The Question of Purpose

The case method serves a variety of teaching objectives, some of which may also be served by other teaching materials and approaches. We believe that case teaching speaks to a compelling combination of purposes that argue for its use in a wide range of classroom situations.

Foster Critical Thinking. As we have suggested already, the original purpose of teaching with cases was to develop professional competence: to train the budding lawyer to argue from the principles embedded in the facts and the business executive-to-be to learn to recognize and solve management problems. The aim is now to enlarge such capacities in general, to equip students in many fields, and often no specific field, with a well-founded and well-grounded self-confidence that they can bring to new challenges in a variety of spheres. Thus, a central purpose of case method teaching is to foster analytic or systematic or critical thinking, for both its broad utility and its beneficial role in building up a student's confidence that he or she can deal successfully with unanticipated issues under practical constraints.

Encourage Student Responsibility for Learning. One of the most basic purposes of the case method is to transfer much of the responsibility for learning from the teacher to the student, whose role, as a result, shifts away from passive absorption toward active construction. A student cannot learn much in a case discussion simply by writing down what is said. There is a high correlation between input and output; the student must stay engaged, though not just by talking. Staying engaged means actively responding to the conversation, even internally. To learn from a case discussion, students must formulate and communicate their own ideas and fit the content of the discussion to their own issues and purposes. They cannot sit back and simply receive ideas and information from the teacher to be stored away for some unspecified future use.

Transfer Information, Concept, and Technique. Although many consider case teaching an inefficient way to transfer factual or conceptual material, others assert that it can convey a lot of facts and ideas, including theory, and that it actually strengthens technique. Certainly, a teacher can cover more ground, more of his or her own agenda, by lecturing for an hour and a half than by leading a case discussion of that length. It is less clear that the students will retain the information from a lecture, recognize the concepts in a different context, or apply the correct technique to a new situation. Cases often contain interesting, detailed information about historical events, for example, about organizations and how they work, or about major contemporary issues. Moreover, students associate the information with the story and the experience of working through the issues, which helps them retain it and gives them practice in sorting it. Cases also provide specifics that make concepts, such as those of managerial practice or of political leadership, meaningful. At the same time, discussion challenges students to articulate a conceptual understanding of the facts in a case.

Teachers interested in using cases often ask how they can be used to teach theory. We think that it makes sense to introduce students to the need for theory, and the difficulty of constructing it, by asking them to make sense of what they find in a case. Then, once theory has been presented, cases can give students the opportunity to practice its application and consolidate their learning. We also know teachers who have become concerned about their students' incapacity to apply analytic methods to the unstructured, unlabeled problems of professional life, even after they have studied the methods with lectures, textbooks, and problem sets. These teachers are turning increasingly to cases to build that capacity.

Develop a Command of a Body of Material. The traditional means of motivating students to gain command of a body of material has been the exam. Long, complex cases approach the same goal in a more dynamic manner. Sometimes called research cases, they challenge students to come to class prepared to discuss any aspect of the material, to make connections from one part of it to another, and to separate the relevant from the irrelevant in order to make the job manageable. In some areas, notably medicine, the sheer volume of information is so overwhelming that command of it in the traditional sense is no longer the goal. Here cases are being used to develop the student's capacity for thinking about the subject, setting learning agendas, and acquiring information as it becomes necessary to deal with problems as they arise.

Blend Affective and Cognitive Learning. The case method asks students to venture out into the unstructured complexity of the case and the uncertain experience of the discussion. In grappling with the issues and offering their ideas to the class, they feel, as well as understand, some of the pressures and constraints within the case. Their learning takes place below the neck as well as above it. Discussion calls on both teacher and students to bring themselves, not just their intellects, into the process. Expressing what he or she would do in a particular situation and why, a student puts personal values on the line along with analytic and rhetorical skills. Some of the experience of risk, which comes with problems in the real world, enters the classroom and helps prepare students to take it on outside.

Enliven the Classroom Dynamic. A good case discussion can be an exciting and exhausting experience for both students and teacher. Even short of role-play or simulation, cases can bring an intensity to the classroom capable of engaging even the most diffident student. By their very nature, cases breathe life into the subject, first by rendering it in concrete detail and then by encouraging students to project themselves into the picture. Their active participation, and assumption of responsibility, introduce a multiplicity of voices and a degree of creative tension. Because case problems involve a specific set of facts, disagreements cannot easily dissipate in bloodless intellectual discourse. Engagement in the issues and the conversation raise the stakes. The class comes to resemble more an actual decision-making meeting than an academic debate. At its best, a good case discussion is an authentic participatory experience in a sense that a lecture, no matter how brilliant, can never be.

Develop Collaborative Skills. One of the several ways in which case discussion mirrors professional practice is that it emphasizes individual participation in a collective enterprise. In the classroom as in the outside world, the individual's contribution is necessary but not sufficient. In both, it is influenced by, and in turn affects, the contributions of others. So collaboration shapes the process and also the content of a case discussion. A good one exhibits some degree of synergy: the class product exceeds the sum of the students' individual contributions because it results partly from the interaction among them. Typically, class participation accounts for a significant percentage of the grade a student receives in a case method course. This incentive is helpful especially when it comes with guidance from the teacher and feedback from peers. Partly by explaining what makes effective participation and giving students individual feedback, and partly by challenging the students to build on each other's contributions and saying how they advance the discussion, the teacher can give explicit attention to collaboration skills. By engaging the students in mutual feedback, even in evaluation of each other's participation, the teacher can give still more emphasis to these skills, for example, making one's ideas accessible to the group, facilitating others' thinking and expression, reframing the discussion, and listening to the group and synthesizing its product.

Teach Questioning and Self-Directed Learning. What concerns case teachers, in the end, is that students learn to ask good questions and carry on their own learning, that they acquire the capacity to recognize new issues and explore them skillfully. One of the foremost purposes of case teaching, in fact, is to communicate the critical value of good questions in a world where there are very few single right answers. The emphasis the case method gives to the process of searching for an answer, making that at least as important as finding an answer, is one of its most characteristic features. By the skillful use of questions, the teacher not only directs the discussion but teaches questioning as well. By introducing their own questions and taking responsibility for the inquiry, the students take steps toward learning to direct their own learning.

The Discussion Process

The case method is a highly flexible approach that displays as much variety in the classroom activity as in the teaching materials. There are few rules, but being a collaborative exercise, it requires that both teacher and students keep some fundamental agreements.

Preparation. Far from simply showing up with sharpened pencils and empty notebooks, students have to read the case thoroughly and think about it carefully, reaching conclusions they are willing to advocate, before coming to class. We favor assigning study questions along with the case to help them prepare. Designed for different purposes than questions raised during discussion, these tend to stimulate wide investigation of the problem and its background. For example, one might ask the students to take a retrospective look at the protagonist's actions up to the decision point. Besides doing their own individual preparation, students often meet before class in small groups to compare their thoughts about the case. Teachers do well, especially in classes larger than about thirty students, to encourage the formation of these study groups. They multiply the opportunities for students to express their views, give quieter students the chance to test their perceptions, and create the chance for informal feedback on class participation.

Like the students, the teacher needs to think through the case from his or her own perspective but also to come to class prepared to engage the students and orchestrate their separate and sometimes dissonant voices. What this requires is knowing the territory of the case well enough to orient oneself to its contours and pathways from any point of time, place, or action. Case discussion is less like marching an orderly band of hikers on a predetermined course across the terrain than it is like bringing a scattered group of parachutists into contact from all the random places they have landed. It requires thinking about the class and the students as well as the case; the teacher needs to have a plan for both the process and the content of discussion. Knowing the students—their backgrounds, concerns, assumptions, and habits of thinking—contributes to the process and advances their learning. Thorough familiarity with the material and the students enables the teacher to strive for the ideal of asking the right question of the right student at the right time (Kasulis, 1982).

Participation. Since it is a collaborative exercise, the success of a case discussion largely depends on the students' willingness to engage and participate in it. Their preparation, the case itself, and the teacher's management of the class all have a significant influence on participation. Earlier we discussed several factors that affect student interest in a given case. The students' preparation, besides equipping them with fact and opinion, gives them a stake in the process, a desire to expound their views that balances the risk they take in doing so. Case teachers often assign memos, due at the start of class, in which students present their analyses and recommendations for action. When they develop their ideas to that extent, it has a definite, positive impact on the degree and quality of their participation.

The teacher can support participation in various ways. One way is to orient the students to the discussion and build in some coherence by relating the case to others in the course and outlining the major themes to consider, suggesting, rather than insisting, what the case might be about in general. Another is to address questions to a specific perspective within the case. Much of the energy of participation comes from student identification with the story, and the teacher sometimes needs to bring a bit of theater into the classroom to produce it. By setting the scene, reiterating the protagonist's dilemma, and keeping the discussion grounded in the actual situation, the teacher can encourage students to inhabit the case. Assigning groups of students to speak for different interests within the case, and staging actual role-plays, are ways of intensifying the action perspective even further. These devices fall short of outright simulation, which seems to us another genre of teaching, but they stimulate participation and produce their own fascinating data for discussion.

A role-play can be very simple and impromptu. A student might suggest that, as someone in the case, he or she would make a certain statement to someone else. The teacher might then ask the student to try it out on another student playing the other person. A role-play can also be planned, and somewhat more involved. In a case widely used in public management programs, an administrator has to deal with a small hostile group that barges into her office making demands. After some discussion of what her options are, teachers often ask one student to play her role while several others play the group, giving the student playing the administrator the chance to test some of the options with live antagonists and an audience. In our view, role-plays require debriefing to be effective learning experiences. Students who enact them need to explain what they have experienced; students who observe need to test their perceptions, both with role-players and other observers. The class as a whole has to step back and think collectively about what has been learned. A rough guideline is that at least as much time should be devoted to the debriefing as to the role-play itself.

Ownership. The most basic agreement of the case method is that although the teacher designs the course, assigns the cases, and conducts the class, the discussion belongs to the students in the sense that what they say genuinely matters. Within the structure provided, they expound their own ideas about the case and draw their own conclusions from the discussion. The teacher may add some thoughts to the conversation, especially at the end, but it is not a charade in which the students just say what the teacher thinks. If they are to risk engaging in the issues and take responsibility for learning from the case, the discussion has to reinforce their sense of ownership. Such refinements of discussion-leading as keeping interventions short and recording students' remarks accurately on the board contribute to this sense, but the teacher's primary technique is the use of questions.

Questions. In its purposes as well as its technique, case teaching is really about questions, framing them to initiate, focus, and direct the inquiry carried out by students, and using them to teach inquiry itself. In a case discussion, the question is not a rhetorical device for staging an answer, either to transfer it between teacher and student or to demonstrate that either one of them has it. The "Paper Chase" notwithstanding, it is also not an inquisitorial device intended to intimidate or harass. The point of a question in this context is to stimulate exploration and to generate and reap the rewards of the process of moving toward an answer. And in some sense, the point of a question is not to reach the answer but rather to reach the next question.

By asking open-ended questions rather than making assertions or resorting to leading questions, the case teacher signals that he or she is committed to listening carefully to what the students say, is open to learning, and is not fixed on a rigid class plan. When the students respond with their own ideas, questions become the means to probe, develop, and connect them. They can also be used to advance the discussion process itself, even call attention to it when that serves the group's learning. In an atmosphere of open inquiry, everything that takes place is a possible gateway to a path of questions. The thoughtful case teacher's kit contains a variety of questions he or she can select for different purposes.

With skillful follow-up questions, the teacher can guide the discussion without excluding any comments. An observation that appears to be unrelated, for example, may mean that the student has made a connection that others, including the teacher, have missed. It may also mean that the student, and still others, have missed what some have seen. In either case, gentle questions that probe the comment for its basis and assumptions can reveal the reasoning in a nonthreatening but powerful way that informs everyone. A simple "Why?" is often enough to move a case discussion to a new and deeper level of insight. Exploring the reasoning behind a comment, no matter how misguided it might turn out to be, may lead to insights about what is relevant and what is not, about the influence of assumptions, and about the process of analysis. We know of one teacher, in a largely quantitative course, who gives a prize at the end of the semester for the "best wrong answer," that is, for an idea that proved to be incorrect but provoked a productive discussion that led to that conclusion.

Questions may draw ideas from the whole class as well as bring out an individual's contribution. When one student expresses a view the teacher thinks might not be widely shared, for example, the question "Does everyone agree with that?" provides a simple way of prodding the others to offer their views or take the risk of being misrepresented by their silence. A teacher can also emphasize that learning is both an individual and a collective enterprise by directing a question to a particular student. As the semester moves on, he or she will begin to learn how certain students approach problems, what assumptions they bring to bear, and what positions they are likely to take. It then becomes possible to seek, say, a bold view from one student, or a reflective one from another, when that would seem to advance the discussion.

Listening. The teacher's skillful questioning depends on careful listening, in itself a skill that the process both teaches and requires. Case discussions are continuing conversations; if the work is to be collaborative, comments have to build on one another. Teacher and students all need to listen carefully and respectfully to one another and withhold an intervention, no matter how brilliant, when the conversation has fruitfully gone beyond the point at which it was relevant. But they also need to risk the disruption of a thoughtful intervention when that promises to take the conversation in a more productive direction.

Risk and challenge color the process. Teachers as well as students have to be willing to express themselves and their ideas and listen to their colleagues respond. Case discussions call on students to reveal opinions, assumptions, and values that lie behind their analytic perspectives. They call on teachers to accept that students can teach them something, can point out issues or questions that are new. Commitment to the pursuit of questions is demanding. It often seems easier for the teacher to ask less of the students, and of themselves, to provide answers instead of more questions. We think both the experience of case discussion and the learning that comes with it make the challenge worthwhile.

New Directions

Currently, case teaching is emerging in new content areas, experimenting with new media, and extending the dimensions of process. In taking these new directions, it is making some interesting connections with its roots.

Content. In some sense a derivative of clinical teaching in medicine, the case method has fairly recently moved into the vanguard of preclinical medical education. In the New Pathways curriculum at the Harvard Medical School, and elsewhere, students explore cases in small group tutorials to learn the basic sciences traditionally presented in large lectures. At the same time, case teaching continues to be taken up both in areas where it seems unsurprising and in areas where it still is not widely thought to be appropriate. As an example of the former, teachers in international affairs are gaining exposure to this approach through a project that aims to extend its use in that field. The best example we know of the less obvious application is in the teaching of microeconomics. Cases have recently been developed for basic courses in that subject at the Kennedy School of Government at Harvard and published in a textbook collection. But we have heard, also, of one educator interested in using cases to teach middle school math teachers to think more creatively about that subject.

Media. Cases traditionally appear in the medium that was dominant when they took hold, the written text. Today, video and computer technology come into increasing use, separately and together, both to present cases and to engage students in working through them. Videotapes may simply illustrate the ambience of a case, or they may bring the students face to face with its central figures to hear their viewpoints, complete with the nuances that no brief text can capture. They may also transmit the case as a full-fledged documentary. The computer adds a new dimension, earlier hinted by the calculator, to the interaction between student and case. In written cases, quantitative data have to be presented quite selectively in graphs and tables that make the trends they are intended to convey accessible but not too apparent. Electronic cases, which come on disks instead of paper, can provide much more complete, raw data for the student to explore with a spreadsheet program. Interestingly, by presenting less process data, cases reflect their origins as unedited documents while they give students new means of practicing one of contemporary life's generic tasks, dealing with high volumes of information.

The combination of interactive video and computer technology leads to the most sophisticated case material we have encountered. Here, the student plays one or more key roles in a crisis such as the radiation leak at Three Mile Island, and faces a series of multiple-choice decision points and a constant stream of new developments, frequently dramatized in the sights, sounds, and voices of the actual event displayed on a video monitor. At any point, the student can tap into a critique of his or her action choices that has been prerecorded by faculty and other experts, an intriguing variation on the classroom teacher. Inhabiting the case, clearly a figurative expression in the context of ordinary cases, becomes much more descriptive here. With this kind of material, student activity passes beyond case discussion, even simple role-play, into simulation, though some of the defining features of the case method remain in the picture. Simulation is a more elaborate activity, in which students either play real people or assume real roles and play themselves. Such rich resources and intense involvement offer students an enormous learning opportunity, and it is interesting to consider whether this represents a true departure from the case method, a technical enhancement of the case writer's and teacher's art, or something in between.

Process. One purpose of simulation, as of classroom role-play, is to have students generate caselike data from their own behavior for their own learning. Another way of involving the students more directly, already explored by some case teachers, extends this purpose to the actual classroom behavior of both teacher and students by making the class itself a case in point. Obviously, certain courses lend themselves more easily than others to this technique, for example, those in group dynamics, organizational behavior, leadership, politics, and teaching. What we mean by making the class a case in point is making explicit what is immediately going on in the room, such as miscommunication or tension between different constituencies in the class, which might reflect similar dynamics within a case being discussed. Making it explicit, and making it part of the conversation and learning in the course, is a demanding and sometimes provocative activity. It requires a high level of trust, risk, and candor, and even more than role-play and simulation, it creates a high demand for processing, that is, for discussing what is happening while, or just after, it takes places.

Using the class as case in point circles back to the case method's basic purpose of teaching students to think systematically about, and deal effectively with, their immediate experience. An indication of its fundamental strength is that case teaching expresses so much of its essential character in taking new directions.

References

Bennett, J. B., and Chakravarthy, B. "What Awakens Student Interest in a Case?" *Harvard Business School Bulletin*, 1978, *54* (2), 12–15.

Bouton, C., and Garth, R. Y. (eds.). *Learning in Groups*. New Directions for Teaching and Learning, no. 14. San Francisco: Jossey-Bass, 1983.

Brown, J. S., Collins, A., and Duguid, P. "Situated Cognition and the Culture of Learning." *Educational Researcher*, 1989, *18* (1), 32–42.

Cantor, J. *The Teaching-Learning Process*. New York: Holt, Rinehart & Winston, 1953.

Coles, R. *The Call of Stories: Teaching and the Moral Imagination*. Boston: Houghton Mifflin, 1989.

Erskine, J. A., Leenders, M. R., and Mauffette-Leenders, L. A. *Teaching with Cases*. London, Canada: School of Business Administration, University of Western Ontario, 1981.

Kasulis, T. P. "Questioning." In M. M. Gullette (ed.), *The Art and Craft of Teaching*. Cambridge, Mass.: Harvard-Danforth Center for Teaching and Learning, Harvard University, 1982.

Kraft, R. G. "Bike Riding and the Art of Learning." *Change*, 1978, *10* (6), 36, 40–42.

Towl, A. R. *To Study Administration by Cases*. Boston: Graduate School of Business Administration, Harvard University, 1969.

Whitehead, A. N. *The Aims of Education*. Cambridge, England: Cambridge University Press, 1929.

John Boehrer is a teaching consultant at the Kennedy School of Government, Harvard University, Cambridge, Massachusetts, and director of the Pew Faculty Fellowship in International Affairs.

Marty Linsky is a lecturer in public policy at the Kennedy School of Government.

Providing supplemental instruction in the skills needed to survive in a course does not require extensive external intervention; it can probably best be done by the instructor.

Rescue the Perishing: A New Approach to Supplemental Instruction

Calvin B. Peters

As faculty, we are not infrequently caught in a dilemma of our own device. We have worked diligently to be sure that our courses require students to move to the application of ideas and beyond. We have struggled to write examination questions that do not in the end reduce merely to commands for memorization. Yet we know we have not succeeded. Our students, even our earnest and studious ones, cannot do what we ask, and there does not seem to be anything we can say or do to stem the tide of low grades, except to encourage our classes to be more studious and earnest.

Of course, the dilemma can be resolved through a series of machinations. On exams, we can conspire with students to transform legitimate application questions into memory items by giving away the answers. We can contort our grading schemes to award A's and B's to students who could not apply a memorized principle to new situations if their lives depended on it. We can give outrageously low grades to scores of students and tout that as a sign of a truly college-level course. But none of these "solutions" is very satisfying.

What would be satisfying is a scheme that would allow students to transform their abilities to read texts, to take notes, to study, and to take tests so that they—or many of them—could learn to apply the principles and concepts of a discipline to new situations and problems. I believe such a scheme exists. It requires work on the part of the instructor, but, in the end, it promises to help students learn to think.

The Idea of Supplemental Instruction

In 1983, the *Journal of Higher Education* published the article "Breaking the Attrition Cycle," which outlined a program of "supplemental instruction . . . designed to assist students in mastering course concepts and, at the same time, to increase student competency in reading, reasoning, and study skills" (Blanc, DeBuhr, and Martin, 1983, p. 81). A perusal of the article reveals an operation in which "specialists" (often advanced undergraduates) attend "high-risk courses," take notes, and complete assignments prior to conducting "three or four, fifty-minute supplemental instruction sessions" each week. In these sessions, the specialists concentrate on modeling appropriate "thinking and languaging behavior" (p. 81), and on using the materials of the subject discipline as the vehicle for academic skills instruction.

No tortuous logic is required to see that the supplemental instruction program might offer a satisfying way out of the dilemma described above. Of course, supplemental instruction is well known to many instructional development personnel, thanks to a widely publicized endorsement by the U.S. Department of Education. There is nothing wrong in endorsing supplemental instruction; it is a good idea that deserves praise.

The celebration of supplemental instruction has, however, drawn attention not to the underlying principles that make the idea a good one but rather to the structure described in the *Journal of Higher Education*. The effect of this structural emphasis has, I think, institutionalized a single way of thinking about the idea. Now, when supplemental instruction is mentioned, it is discussed as a particular program, organized and implemented in a particular way.

For some campuses, this emphasis on the programmatic aspects of supplemental instruction is not a problem. They have the resources necessary to duplicate the now standard, specialist-centered program of supplemental instruction. Unfortunately, for most of us, supplemental instruction in its full-blown, programmatic form is simply not feasible. We do not have the resources, we do not have specialists, and we do not have any hope of acquiring them. A program of supplemental instruction is for us only a hope that, like so many in the academic world, begins with "If only we had more. . . ."

All of this is true only so long as supplemental instruction is conceived as a program rather than an idea. What makes supplemental instruction work is not the particular structure in which it first appeared but rather the principle of using materials from your course to provide your students organized practice in the academic skills most necessary for them to succeed in your grading system. Obviously, if it is to be employed, this principle requires some structure, but it does not have to depend on specialists, and it does not have to be expensive. So, for those of you who find the idea of supplemental instruction attractive, but who also find the program prohibitively costly and complex, what follows is an alternative—in short, supplemental instruction on the cheap.

Preliminary Considerations

Before beginning even a cheap supplemental instruction program, you should first be sure that your course requires students to do more than memorize the texts and the wisdom you dispense in your lectures. This is often not easy to do. Old habits are hard to break, and the habit of asking students to recapitulate your own comparisons and contrasts, your own explanations, and your own projections of the consequences of various theories is one of the most tenacious. If you want students to do a better job in memorizing instruction on what you and designated authors have said, do not bother with supplemental instruction; just be clearer about what it is that you want them to know.

Second, you should be sure you know what you are getting into. Supplemental instruction is not a fancy substitute for standard "help sessions." It is not designed merely to review lectures, to answer questions, and to clarify fuzzy thinking. It is, rather, designed to provide instruction in academic skills (for example, text reading, note taking, studying, examination taking) in a context tailor-made for a specific course. Although "standard" review may constitute a part of supplemental instruction sessions, the development of skills should remain paramount.

In the specialist-centered, deluxe program of supplemental instruction, this distinction between review and skills development must be maintained by the specialist responsible for the conduct of the sessions. If you are doing supplemental instruction on the cheap, you are the specialist. This may, in fact, be an improvement. Who better to model academic skills on course material? Who better to create realistic practice settings? Who better to see to it that the sessions focus on skills and application and not on recitation and memory?

Once you have sorted through your course and decided that supplemental instruction is for you (and this is not a decision that should be made lightly because there is considerable work connected to it), you then need to focus your efforts on specific skills. The rubric of "academic skills" is not sufficiently narrow to allow you to construct coherent, manageable sessions.

The best way to identify particular skills on which to focus your supplemental instruction sessions is to work your way through what you expect your students to do. Most of us expect them to read books, to listen to lectures, and to take examinations after preparing for them. If you concentrate on the text-reading, note-taking, studying, and examination-taking skills necessary for those activities, you will not go wrong.

Remember some of the more common comments from students (usually made with an inflection that cannot be transcribed): "I don't understand the reading; the book is too hard"; "I can't follow you when you lecture"; "I study the wrong things"; "I can't take the kinds of tests you give; they don't test what I know."

These sessions devoted to particular skills define another one of the differences between deluxe supplemental instruction and the on-the-cheap version. When you cannot have three or four sessions a week (and if you are the one doing them, you probably cannot), you need to plan to spend your time most effectively. By focusing entire sessions on particular skills, you can pay some concentrated attention to the skills that are most important for students' success in your course.

Timing and Structure

The timing of the introduction and conduct of supplemental instruction sessions is crucial to their success. If you want your supplemental instruction to be most effective, you will need to start it as near to the beginning of the semester as possible. Each student in your course has a set of study skills. If you let them unpack those skills and begin to use them, all your warnings about how different your course is from the others they have had will fall on deaf ears. By scheduling your set of supplemental instruction sessions in the first two weeks of the semester, you can give substance to your claims that there is something more than memorization to be done in your course. Further, if the sessions are held early in the semester, students tend to perceive them as a normal (and almost expected) part of the course. There is none of the stigma that often attaches to workshops, help sessions, and the like conducted because "a lot of you didn't do well on the first exam." All of this works together to convince them that you might be serious when you say that "you can't succeed in this course by memorizing."

The sessions themselves depend for their success on three general principles. The first is the most important. The workshops, as the name implies, should be *active*. Do not let your students just sit there and take notes on what you say, even if the skill you plan to cover is note taking. What you hope they take away from the workshop is a set of new ways of doing things, not a list of things that would be good to do. If they are going to learn how to study, how to take examinations, how to take notes, how to read texts, they are going to have to engage in those activities. Lists of principles are fine. In fact, you should probably try to develop some as summaries to be distributed at the end of the workshops. But, by themselves, the principles, no matter how cogent, will not do. They must be derived from activity if they are to do the job.

Of course, not just any activity will suffice. This brings up the second principle. Your workshops should *simulate* the actual conditions under which your students labor. Do not give them a list of principles of text reading; give them a list of principles that apply to the specific texts assigned in your course. Do not engage them in note taking from a packaged lecture; engage them in note taking from a videotape of a lecture you have just given in class. This is the heart of the idea. Your workshops are designed to encourage the development in students of study skills that will allow them to succeed in your course. Those skills are best developed through the active use of the materials from your course. Use *your* texts, use *your* lectures, use *your* examinations. If you do not, give up your workshops altogether, since workshops using generic material are already held at the local Learning Assistance Center.

There is no reason to go to the trouble to conduct workshops if you do not give your students a chance to put the study skills to work. This is the third principle: your workshops should give students plenty of opportunities to *practice* on real, live course material. Have them study for an examination. Give them the exam. Review it with them. Give them a chance to restudy. Give them a comparable exam, and so on. Whatever you do, give your students an opportunity to practice what you have been preaching.

A Sample Session

Let me illustrate just how these principles can be put into practice. I usually conduct four workshops for my students sometime in the first two weeks of the semester. The most important is, I believe, the one devoted to studying. Even with the best notes in the world, a clear idea of the reading, and freshly honed test-taking skills, a student who has no idea of how to put those things together in a meaningful way is simply not going to succeed.

My studying workshop is usually the third in the series, and as such it follows the format established by the first two. The students come expecting to do some studying. And that is precisely what I ask them to do. Using the same excerpt from their text that I used in the reading workshop, I ask them to take five or ten minutes to study the material. The realism of the situation is heightened by the fact that at the conclusion of their study time I tell them that there will be a short, three-question test. I have reproduced the excerpt (Freud, 1961, p. 33) below, and it might be fun for you to duplicate the exercise as you read this article.

> Our enquiry concerning happiness has not so far taught us much that is not already common knowledge. And even if we proceed from it to the problem of why it is so hard for men to be happy, there seems no

greater prospect of learning anything new. We have given the answer already by pointing to three sources from which our suffering comes: the superior power of nature, the feebleness of our own bodies and the inadequacy of the regulations which adjust the mutual relationships of human beings in the family, the state and society. In regard to the first two sources, our judgment cannot hesitate long. It forces us to acknowledge those sources of suffering and to submit to the inevitable. We shall never completely master nature; and our bodily organism, itself a part of that nature, will always remain a transient structure with a limited capacity for adaptation and achievement. This recognition does not have a paralyzing effect. On the contrary, it points the direction for our activity. If we cannot remove all suffering, we can remove some, and we can mitigate some: the experience of many thousands of years has convinced us of that. As regards the third source, the social source of suffering, our attitude is a different one. We do not admit it at all; we cannot see why the regulations made by ourselves should not on the contrary, be a protection and benefit for every one of us. And yet, when we consider how unsuccessful we have been in precisely this field of prevention of suffering, a suspicion dawns on us that here, too, a piece of unconquerable nature may lie behind—this time a piece of our own psychical constitution.

When we start considering this possibility, we come upon a contention which is so astonishing that we must dwell upon it. This contention holds that what we call our civilization is largely responsible for our misery, and that we should be much happier if we gave it up and returned to primitive conditions. I call this contention astonishing because, in whatever way we may define the concept of civilization, it is a certain fact that all the things with which we seek to protect ourselves against the threats that emanate from the sources of suffering are part of that very civilization.

Are you ready for the examination? Most of my students, as is probably the case with those of you who are playing along at home, say that they think so, but they are a little nervous because they do not know exactly what is going to be on the test. It is a perfect simulation of the situation that obtains when the first real exam is given in the course. Without further ado, the test:

Exam I

1. What are the three sources from which human suffering comes?
2. Which of the sources of human suffering seems most likely to be controlled by human effort?

3. In which conditions, primitive or civilized, does Freud believe we would be happier?

So, how did you do? Was the test hard? Easy? As you might guess, after I review the answers, most students discover they did well on this examination. It is precisely the kind of thing they know how to prepare for. The questions are drawn directly from the reading, and they require nothing more advanced than memory. The students know that. With a little prompting, they will tell me that the test was "easy because it was all right there and we just had to memorize it."

At this point, when they are flushed with success, I remind them that for my course memorization is not the most important skill. With that as the only hint, I tell them that they have five more minutes to study for another examination with three new questions of a different kind. In they plunge; they still know what to do. Take the same five minutes and get ready for Exam II.

Exam II

1. Freud believes that some of our suffering is inevitable. Explain the logic behind Freud's belief.
2. The "human source" of suffering, Freud says, cannot be "admitted at all." What is the meaning of this claim?
3. Freud claims that we would be happier if we "abandoned" civilization. Explain the reasons behind this "astonishing" claim.

They do not do quite so well on this examination, but still the performance of the group is good. Of course, they say this examination is harder than the first one, and they suspect that it is this sort of question that will appear on the first real exam in a week or two. When I ask them what they had to do to prepare for this test, they say things like "you really had to know it" or "you couldn't just memorize, you had to understand it." They are not at a loss. They know how to prepare for this sort of question. They may not like the difficulty of the question, but they know how to answer it.

This is the critical point in the workshop. Exam II is probably harder than Exam I, but it does not require students to do anything other than memorize in order to succeed. They now commit to memory connections that Freud makes in the text (or that most likely would be made by a lecturer in class) instead of isolated bits of information. Nonetheless, they memorize. What they must memorize differs, but the intellectual skill involved remains the same. The point is not lost on them. The two exams test the same content and the same skill: memory. Exam II may require students to memorize more important material, but the three answers to the questions can be supplied by rote.

Again, that is not the skill I am interested in having my students develop. So, I tell them that they have a few more minutes and then there will be yet another exam, over the same material, with three questions of still another type. Now they have run out of ideas and patience (as you must be). "Just give us the test," they say. Okay, here goes.

Exam III

1. Advances in medicine promise to relieve pain and suffering and to prolong human life. Explain how Freud would react to a statement that these sorts of advances promise to eliminate the suffering that comes "from the feebleness of our own bodies."
2. A claim is made that society, if it is just, with equal opportunity for all, can produce satisfied and happy individuals. How would Freud respond to such a claim?
3. A sociologist claims that because of modern conveniences and technological advances, citizens in the industrial world are better off than members of "primitive" civilizations. How would Freud respond to this idea?

What is different about these questions? They are not in the reading, you cannot memorize the answers, and, ultimately, the students say, you cannot study for them. But, of course, what they mean is that there is nothing to memorize, and because memorizing is studying, well, there is no way to prepare. By now they have figured out that the sort of question that I intend to ask is the kind on Exam III. They also have some idea of the kind of preparation that will not be productive when they sit down to study. And that is not bad, especially because they have discovered it in an active way in a situation enough like their real classroom experiences to be meaningful.

I close the session by trying to crystallize what steps I think are useful in studying Freud, and then I distribute a printed set of "Hints on Studying Freud." By themselves, I do not believe these study hints are particularly useful. Placed in the context of this workshop, illustrated by a little modeling on my part and a little practice on theirs, the hints seem to work reasonably well.

By using the principles listed above and the outlines of the studying workshop as a rough blueprint, it should be relatively easy to design productive workshop sessions. If the "modeling" mentioned in the discussion of deluxe supplemental instruction is added to them, you have the makings of a top-notch, on-the-cheap program. They try, you model. They try again, you discuss principles. You model, they practice. The process works like a charm.

Thoughts on the Future

Speaking of working, does all of this (any of this) work? It is hard to tell. The results reported in the *Journal of Higher Education* indicate that the deluxe version works spectacularly. There are no comparable figures for the on-the-cheap model, but, if my own experience is any guide, it is safe to say that the cheap version works, if not spectacularly, at least very well. Students report overwhelmingly that the sessions are beneficial, and their behavior is consistent with that claim. They sample the sessions, and continue to attend. They even bring their friends.

Because of this effectiveness, there is, I think, a temptation to drop the "supplemental" from this sort of instruction and to integrate it into regular class sessions. I have resisted doing this for two reasons. First, not surprisingly, is the issue of coverage. The four sessions I conduct last a cumulative six hours. Further, though the workshops do use course material, and therefore do provide some review of course content, they are expressly devoted to skill development. If that time is removed from the class sessions that remain after those several periods devoted to examinations are subtracted, I would have to choose to drop course material in order to develop skills. Happily, when the sessions are supplemental, that is a choice that does not have to be made.

Second, I believe the supplemental character of the workshop has a salutary effect on students' perceptions of the course and what they need to do in order to succeed. It is clear to them from the workshops that the course demands something different from rote memorization. It is also clear to them that their instructor recognizes his responsibility to provide students the support they require. The fact that I (and not some third-party specialist) conduct these supplemental workshops demonstrates in a way that ample office hours do not that I am willing to work outside of class to help them develop the skills they need to succeed in class. This message makes its mark on them.

For several reasons, supplemental instruction is clearly an idea whose time has come. As colleges and universities expand their search for students in response to a declining population of high school graduates, faculty are increasingly likely to confront classrooms populated by students whose academic skills are inadequate to the tasks at hand. Supplemental instruction seems tailor-made for this situation: it provides students assistance in skill development without consigning them to remedial courses, and at the same time it provides instructors with a way to make their courses accessible to students without lowering standards or "spoon feeding" information.

In another way, however, supplemental instruction seems distinctly out of step with the movement of American higher education. Effective supplemental instruction (in either its "expensive" or "cheap" incarnation) depends on faculty who are willing to think about what skills are important for students' success in their courses, and who are willing to invest time and energy in designing and conducting supplemental activities to foster those skills. Given the steady expansion of the role that refereed publications and external funding play in promotion and tenure decisions, it is difficult to imagine that any significant number of faculty are going to make any additional investment of time and energy in their teaching.

It is ironic that in mitigating one dilemma supplemental instruction exacerbates another, more perplexing one. How are faculty to choose between their careers and investment in students, between their sense of self-worth and attention to students' needs, especially when the choice is between time for research and time for a successful instructional activity? The future of supplemental instruction, like teaching itself, rests on the choices faculty and the institutions that house them make in this regard.

References

Blanc, R. A., DeBuhr, L. E., and Martin, D. C. "Breaking the Attrition Cycle." *Journal of Higher Education*, 1983, *54*, 80–89.
Freud, S. *Civilization and Its Discontents.* New York: Norton, 1961.

Calvin B. Peters is an associate professor of sociology and anthropology at the University of Rhode Island, Kingston.

PART TWO

Changing Perspectives

By becoming skilled assessors of their students' learning,
faculty can improve the quality of higher education where
it matters most—in their own classrooms.

Classroom Assessment: Improving Learning Quality Where It Matters Most

Thomas A. Angelo

The purpose of this chapter is fivefold. First, it argues that if we are to improve the quality of higher education in the 1990s, individual college teachers will need to become more skilled assessors of student learning in their own classrooms. Next, it aims to define Classroom Assessment, as Angelo and Cross have developed it, and to contrast it with traditional classroom testing and evaluation. Third, it outlines the steps faculty take in planning and carrying out their first Classroom Assessment projects. Fourth, it attempts to illustrate the definition with three examples of simple faculty projects. Lastly, it places Classroom Assessment within the broader framework of Classroom Research.

Introduction

There was a lot of agitation for reform of higher education during the 1980s, most of it focused on the system, campus, or program level and mandated from the top down. Assessment, a term applied to a wide range of approaches used to measure educational effectiveness, became a cornerstone of the movement. But the types and purposes of these assessments focused on asking *what* and *how much* (or how little) students knew at point A or had learned between points A and B. By contrast, comparatively little attention was paid to assessing *how* and *how well* students were learning or to identifying which factors most directly influence the quality of student learning in the classroom.

Yet, it is in the thousands of college classrooms across the nation that the fundamental work of higher education, teaching and learning, takes place. If assessment is to substantively improve the quality of student learning, and not just provide greater accountability, both faculty and students must become personally invested and actively involved in the process. One way to involve them is to build a complementary, micro-level, grass-roots assessment movement. Classroom Assessment aims to do just that by developing methods to bring the benefits of assessment into individual classrooms and under the control of individual teachers and learners.

Classroom Assessment: What It Is

Classroom Assessment is a straightforward, learner-centered, teacher-directed approach that makes use of assessment to improve the effectiveness of higher education where it matters most: in the college classroom. Classroom Assessment assumes that one of the most promising ways to improve learning quality is to encourage and enable faculty members to develop the expertise to assess the effects of their teaching on student learning.

In January 1988, with support from the Pew Charitable Trusts and the Ford Foundation, Professor K. Patricia Cross and I began the Classroom Research Project to develop and disseminate the methods and materials college teachers need to become Classroom Researchers—independent, systematic, and effective inquirers into the dynamics of their students' learning.

Classroom Assessment is the most highly developed element thus far in the broader Classroom Research approach. Classroom Assessment, as we envision it, is an integrated approach to instructional dev lopment consisting of three components.

The first component of Classroom Assessment is the Teaching Goals Inventory, a brief, self-scoreable questionnaire that helps teachers identify and clarify their teaching goals as the first step toward assessing them. A second element of this component is a kind of tool kit, a collection of simple and flexible Classroom Assessment Techniques (CATs), which faculty adapt and apply to determine how well they are meeting their instructional goals (Cross and Angelo, 1988).

The second component of the project is a one-day training workshop to prepare disciplinary faculty to carry out simple Classroom Assessment projects in their own classes. To date, more than three hundred faculty on a dozen campuses have participated in this workshop. In addition, to foster the development of on-campus training capacity, the project offers two-day, intensive training workshops for faculty developers and academic administrators from colleges interested in implementing their own Classroom Assessment programs. More than two hundred instructional leaders from across the country have participated in these two-day training sessions.

Third, the Classroom Research Project has developed a flexible model for organizing and implementing Classroom Assessment programs on individual campuses. In the course of two years of pilot projects, carried out on two- and four-year campuses, we have learned that to be most effective, faculty training in Classroom Assessment must take place within a well-planned semester- or year-long program of whole group, small group, and two-person activities.

While Classroom Assessment can be practiced in isolation, it rarely is. Experience has convinced us that, within an organized framework, the participating faculty benefit from discussing and working together to assess and improve teaching and learning in their classrooms. As with students, active collaboration enhances faculty learning. The project's organizational model capitalizes on the power of collaborative learning by bringing together faculty within and across departments and disciplines to share insights and expertise.

Through practice in Classroom Assessment, faculty become better able to understand and promote learning, and they increase their ability to help the students themselves become more effective, self-assessing, self-directed learners. Simply put, the central goal of Classroom Assessment, as well as of Classroom Research, is to empower both teachers and their students to improve the quality of what they learn.

The Need for Classroom Assessment: Case-in-Point 1

An anecdote from my own teaching illustrates the need for Classroom Assessment and, in a modest way, its usefulness. I invite you to search your memory for analogous examples from your own experiences as teachers and as students.

This year I am co-teaching a required statistics course in which my colleague lectures and I direct the lab sessions. Whenever possible, I attend my partner's lectures in order to better focus the labs. Recently, he gave an excellent lecture on a particularly tough concept and its applications. He did a masterful job of covering the material. Had I been an outside evaluator rating his teaching, I would have given him high marks for preparation, organization, clarity, and enthusiasm.

I observed our students during his lecture and their vital signs were all healthy. They looked attentive, took notes, nodded and smiled, and even asked a few questions. By the end of the hour, I was convinced that the class had gone very well and that the lab would be smooth sailing.

I began the lab session, as I often do, with a simple Classroom Assessment exercise designed to prompt review of the lecture material. This technique, called RSQC2, gets students to recall the major points of the lecture, summarize those points in one or two sentences, raise questions, comment on how they felt during the lecture, and connect the lecture content to previous class topics (Cross and Angelo, 1988, pp. 152–154). Students write their responses on an index card. Some days, we discuss the responses immediately; on others, I collect the anonymous feedback, read it after lab, and discuss it with students in the subsequent session.

On the particular day in question, I decided to take ten or fifteen minutes from the two-hour session to listen to their RSQC2 responses. So, after they had quickly jotted down answers, I asked for volunteers to respond to each prompt. We started by making a list on the board of the major points they recalled from the lecture. It was, much to my surprise, a disaster. Within sixty seconds, I became convinced that my students and I had not attended the same lecture. They recalled minor points but left out major ones, misrecalled and distorted others, and listed several points that had not even been mentioned in class.

I made a quick decision to skip the summaries and postpone the questions, heading directly for the comments. In response to my prompt of "write one or two adjectives that describe how you were feeling during the lecture," students volunteered "dumb," "frustrated," "lost," "bewildered and anxious," "pressured and upset," and the like. At that moment, I was beginning to empathize with them. My confidence that the lecture had been a success turned out to have been ill-founded.

Further discussion revealed that most of the class had gotten lost early in the lecture but, assuming that things would soon get clearer, they had gone on furiously taking notes. As the moments passed, they had understood less and less, until they no longer even knew what to ask. By the end of the lecture, they were stunned into silence.

This vignette, fortunately, has a happy ending. With some probing, we were able to retrace our steps and pick up the lost trail. My colleague agreed to take the time to review and discuss the previously taught but as yet unlearned points, and almost everyone got them the second time around. Not only did the students learn better after the assessment, they also felt better. They reported feeling more confident and less anxious, and they appreciated our willingness to ask, listen, and respond.

When I first shared the class's responses with my co-teacher, he was as surprised and mystified as I had been. We both had assumed that the students' obvious attentiveness and diligent note taking meant they understood the lecture. We both were wrong. Our momentary chagrin at misdiagnosing the class was soon overcome as we turned to the questions of what to do to get back on track and how to avoid future derailings.

The lesson I draw from this anecdote is a simple one. While learning can and often does take place without the benefit of teaching—or in spite of it—teaching does not happen in the absence of learning. Teaching without learning is just talking. It is common practice, nonetheless, for faculty to assume that when we are at the front of the room talking, our students are learning what we think we are teaching. When it comes time to grade tests and term papers, we are often faced with disconfirming evidence. By that point in the term, however, it is usually too late to remedy the problem. The purpose of Classroom Assessment is to discover gaps between what we teach and what our students learn early enough to close, or at least narrow, those gaps.

Why Faculty Need Explicit Training to Assess Student Learning

While all college teachers gather information on their students' learning, very few do so systematically and regularly enough to use that feedback to help students improve the quality of their learning. Much of the information college teachers collect is used to sort and grade students at the end of units or courses. Such assessment for grading and sorting is known as summative assessment or evaluation. As former undergraduate and graduate students, most faculty have had many years of exposure to classroom tests, quizzes, and term papers by the time they take up the chalk. And even though they may lack technical skills useful in developing and assessing tests and exams, most college teachers are familiar with and capable of becoming skilled at summative assessment in their disciplines.

The great majority of college faculty are less skilled, however, at formative assessment, at getting information early and regularly enough to avoid or defuse learning problems and to help students stay on track. Experienced teachers monitor and react to students' questions, comments made during class discussions, and body language and facial expressions in an almost automatic fashion as they are teaching. This automatic information gathering and impression formation is largely an unconscious and implicit process. Teachers depend on their impressions of student learning and make important judgments based on them, but they rarely make them explicit in order to check their on-line assessments against the students' own impressions or abilities to perform. Most college faculty assume a great deal about their students' learning, and most of those assumptions remain untested.

At the same time, the bulk of the feedback that experienced teachers depend on to make ongoing assessments of student learning and on-line, lightning-fast adjustments in their teaching is diffuse and quickly lost. Since classroom interactions are very complex and of limited duration, few teachers can recall much about them after a class session is over. Much of the classroom data that could inform teaching does not do so simply because the information is not systematically collected, analyzed, or used.

How Faculty Learn to Do Classroom Assessment: An Overview

One purpose common to all Classroom Research programs is to help teachers develop simple ways to investigate, document, and analyze student learning in progress. To do this, teachers have to learn to focus and control the amount and type of feedback they gather on their students' learning. To that end, the Classroom Research Project offers participating faculty a step-by-step process for learning to carry out simple Classroom Assessment projects.

Over the course of a semester, participating faculty work through a ten-step process known as the Classroom Assessment Project Cycle. Though the following list of steps may make the cycle seem daunting, it is meant to be and usually is a simple, relatively quick process to carry out. If we include the eight-hour initial training workshop and a suggested ninety-minute follow-up meeting in the total, the average time an individual teacher spends working through this cycle adds up to about twelve hours spread over several weeks. In the Classroom Assessment Project Cycle, the leaders of campus programs help participating faculty as they

1. Choose one class to focus on, a class that presents teaching/learning problems or questions that are challenging but probably tractable;
2. Identify and clarify critical teaching/learning goals for that "focus" class;
3. Adapt or develop simple techniques for assessing one of those critical goals and plan a simple Classroom Assessment project;
4. Teach to the goal that is being assessed;
5. Assess student achievement of that goal by carrying out the planned project and collecting data;
6. Analyze (study) the data collected through the assessment project;
7. Interpret the results of the data analysis and their implications for future teaching and learning in the class;
8. Plan an educationally appropriate response to the feedback;
9. Tell the students what the results are and what the planned response is; and, if it seems useful,
10. Start the cycle over to assess the effectiveness of the response.

Although faculty are free to carry out their projects independently, almost none of them have chosen to do so. Over and over, participants report that the discussion of teaching and learning problems with their colleagues, particularly those from their own departments, is one of the most valuable outcomes of the program. The most effective initial working arrangements to date have involved pairs and small teams of teachers from the same or like disciplines. Since scheduling meetings is often difficult, pairs and threesomes find it easier to meet as needed to discuss and assist each other during the early stages of their projects. Once most participants on a given campus have completed a project cycle, the whole group convenes for reporting on it. By this stage, several weeks into the process, faculty from various disciplines are usually ready and eager to learn from each other and are able to draw useful analogies among projects and problems in different fields.

A Closer Look at Identifying and Clarifying Teaching Goals

All effective assessments begin with goals. Therefore, before faculty can assess how well their students are learning, they must identify and clarify what it is they are trying to teach. This seems straightforward enough, and, indeed, most faculty can say what it is they are trying to teach when asked. The problem lies in the kind of answers they give. College faculty tend to define their instructional goals in terms of content. When asked, "What are your teaching goals for this class?" most college teachers will say something like, "My goal is to teach linear algebra," or "I'm trying to teach the nineteenth-century British novel."

It usually takes hard thinking before teachers can articulate the specific skills and competencies they hope to teach through the course content. After reconsidering the question, they give answers like, "I want to help my students learn to define and solve real-world problems in engineering and physics that require the application of linear algebra," or "I want to help my students develop an informed, critical appreciation of nineteenth-century British literature and to foster the kind of thoughtful reading that they can enjoy throughout their lives."

Although broadly drawn, such revised goals help faculty see what drives their choice of course content or, at least, what ought to. These instructional goals, focusing on how students will change if they learn, can be further limited and clarified until they are actually assessable.

There are many ways to help teachers identify and clarify their instructional goals so that they can assess their effectiveness in achieving them. The Classroom Research Project has developed a way to do this in less than an hour, using the Teaching Goals Inventory. This exercise requires faculty to identify and rank their instructional goals for a single course. Participating teachers then focus on assessing one important teaching/learning goal from that course. While no attempt is made to influence the choice of a focus goal, many more teachers have focused on skill- or process-related goals than on goals concerned with specific course content. Even though the goals on the inventory are phrased very broadly, in order to be applicable across disciplines, they serve as useful starting points for discussion and for the inevitable revising and personalizing of goals that must precede assessment.

The Importance of Clarifying Teaching Goals: Case-in-Point 2

An engineering instructor recently persuaded five of his colleagues who teach thermodynamics, a required course, to join him in filling out the Teaching Goals Inventory in relation to that course. He then collected the inventory forms and tabulated their responses. Much to his surprise, he found that there was not one goal among the forty-eight on the inventory that all six of them considered essential to the course. Furthermore, the number of goals that faculty rated as essential varied from a low of zero to a high of eight. While there were some areas of overlap, the degree of variance among their lists of essential teaching goals was large.

He and his colleagues found these differences in teaching goals quite striking, especially given that the thermodynamics faculty had just completed a year-long series of discussions leading to the selection of a common text and the creation of a common final exam for the course. These six engineering teachers were at a loss to explain how they could have agreed on the content of the course and on its final evaluation without agreeing on its underlying teaching/learning goals.

Each of the six thermodynamics instructors devoted ten to fifteen minutes to filling out the inventory. It took one of them approximately an hour to tabulate and analyze that data. Thus, a total group investment of less than three hours provided them with challenging but valuable insights into their teaching goals, and a starting point for many productive discussions.

A Closer Look at Classroom Assessment Techniques

Once faculty members have selected specific teaching goals to assess, they determine what kinds of feedback on student learning related to those goals they can quickly and easily collect. Next, they identify techniques they might use to get that information, for example, the RSQC2 method described earlier. Many participants begin by adapting an assessment technique from Cross and Angelo (1988). They are strongly encouraged, however, to design and field-test assessments of their own techniques specially tailored to fit their particular disciplines, syllabi, teaching styles, and students. Consequently, after modeling their first assessment techniques on those in Cross and Angelo (1988), a number of teachers have gone on to create their own ingenious, discipline-specific feedback devices.

The most useful Classroom Assessment Techniques are the following:

1. Context-specific, providing information about what a specific group of students is learning at a given moment in a particular classroom about a specific subject;
2. Action-oriented, focusing on aspects of learner or teacher behavior that can be changed within the limits of time and energy available;
3. Mutually beneficial, giving students information that they can use to improve their learning as well as providing teachers with information to improve their teaching;
4. Formative, not summative, in nature, meaning that they are ungraded and often anonymous assessments used to understand and improve student learning, not to evaluate or sort students;
5. Relatively simple to prepare and easily adaptable to a variety of situations;
6. Quick to administer, yielding data that can be quickly analyzed and turned into information that can be used to improve learning; and,
7. Educationally valid, reinforcing learning of the skills and/or content that are the focus of the course.

Simplicity is a major emphasis throughout Classroom Assessment training. Teachers are urged to adapt and develop simple, appropriate techniques for collecting feedback, to collect no more data than can be turned into useful information, and to use the simplest methods of analyzing the data that can adequately answer their questions. Keeping Classroom Assessment simple minimizes the time and energy it requires, an important concern if busy faculty members are to use the approach regularly.

Since the point of these assessments is to get feedback in order to better fit teaching to learning, it is rarely useful and virtually never necessary to use sophisticated statistical analyses. In fact, since statistical analyses of small, nonrandom samples are inherently problematic, and since the participating teachers are not trying to generalize from their samples to larger populations, such complex analyses are likely to be a waste of time. In Classroom Assessment, the sample is the population, and the purpose is to improve the very class on which the assessment is carried out.

Three Examples of Successful Classroom Assessment Projects

The following three "thumbnail sketches" illustrate the kinds of simple Classroom Assessment projects that faculty can design and carry out. They are also intended to stimulate you to imagine similar assessments that might be useful in your classes.

Example One: Assessing Students' Self-Awareness. An English professor had never felt quite sure what her students were learning from small group work in her composition course. At the end of a group work session devoted to critiquing one another's drafts, she asked her students to write brief, anonymous answers to the following two questions: (1) What did you learn today from the others in your group that will help you improve your writing? (2) How did you help the others in your group to improve their writing?

She was fascinated by their responses but concerned that many of the students could not respond to the second question. The class discussed the assessment the following session, and she noted they gave much more attention and effort to the next group critique. In their second assessment, using the same questions, their responses were more complete and more specific. The instructor reported that both process (the group critiquing sessions) and product (the quality of final drafts) improved noticeably. The experience also convinced her of the need to be much more explicit about her reasons for giving assignments.

Example Two: Assessing Applications of Course Knowledge. A veteran psychology teacher decided to ask his students a question that he had always wondered about, one that concerned his most fundamental goals. After completing a three-week-long unit on human learning in his introductory survey course, he asked students to write a one-page response to this question: Have you applied anything you learned in this unit to your own life? If yes, please give as many specific, detailed examples as possible of those applications.

To his astonishment, twenty-two of the thirty-five students not only said yes but also were able to give convincing examples. Several of the students who said no indicated that they did not realize they were expected to try to apply what they had learned in class! He held a discussion on the question during the next class and invited students to suggest as many possible applications as they could dream up. Participation was extremely high, and he has subsequently built explicit discussion of applications into each major unit.

Example Three: Assessing Students' Goals. A dance instructor wondered why attendance in her large aerobics classes always dropped off sharply over the semester. She decided to ask students to list their five most important goals in taking the course—what they hoped to learn, in other words—and how they hoped to benefit. She then asked them to rank their goals in terms of relative importance and in terms of relative difficulty to achieve. While they listed and ranked their goals, she did the same for hers. She then collected the index cards and took them home to analyze.

Much to her surprise, most of her students were not taking aerobics primarily to get in shape or lose weight, although many mentioned these goals. Their highest-priority goals were to improve self-image and to reduce stress. The instructor recognized that, as a professional dancer herself, she had been teaching the class in a way that many students, given their expressed goals, would find stressful and perhaps even threatening to their self-images. The ensuing class discussion convinced her to rethink her course goals and demonstrated her concern to the students. Not incidentally, perhaps, attendance and retention improved that semester.

The Bigger Picture: From Classroom Assessment to Classroom Research

The participants in our pilot project, more than one hundred faculty from four community colleges and two private four-year colleges, have generally been interested in broader teaching and learning questions than a single Classroom Assessment project can answer. Therefore, once participants feel comfortable with Classroom Assessment, they are encouraged to design more thorough and longer-term projects to study the larger questions. These more ambitious projects, some of which continue for a year or more, represent true Classroom Research efforts. As such, they often incorporate Cross and Angelo's (1988) Classroom Assessment Techniques, but they always go beyond them to include interviewing, videotaping, surveys, and the like. In this way, Classroom Research becomes more than the sum of discrete Classroom Assessment projects. It is the continuous, ongoing, developing study of teaching and learning in the classroom through a wide variety of appropriate, teacher-developed means.

Classroom Assessment happens to be the most clearly elaborated element of Classroom Research to date, but there are many other ways to learn about student learning in the classroom that need to be explored. For example, Classroom Researchers could mine the rich information on development of critical and creative thinking that is buried in classroom tests, homework assignments, term papers, and problem sets. They could develop more effective ways to use focus groups and simulations to assess the effects of course activities on beliefs, values, and dispositions. To fulfill its promise, Classroom Research must become a vehicle for understanding and improving the entire range of learning goals that college teachers have for their students, and that students have for themselves.

The learning that can be improved through this type of action research is not just that of our students, however. By questioning our assumptions and investigating what is and is not happening in our classrooms, we faculty can learn a great deal about student learning, about our teaching, and about how to improve both within our respective fields. And if we pursue these applied research questions systematically across many disciplines and share what we learn, Classroom Researchers can help construct a knowledge base to improve the entire art and science of college teaching. Even the simplest Classroom Assessment Techniques, however, can provide teachers with useful and frequently fascinating information on how students learn in their courses. This information allows teachers to improve their effectiveness. By practicing Classroom Assessment, college teachers take an important first step in harnessing the power of assessment to the task of improving learning quality where it matters most—in their own classrooms.

Reference

Cross, K. P., and Angelo, T. A. *Classroom Assessment Techniques: A Handbook for Faculty.* Ann Arbor: National Center for Research to Improve Postsecondary Teaching and Learning, University of Michigan, 1988.

Thomas A. Angelo is the assistant director of the Classroom Research Project at the University of California, Berkeley.

*Teaching is only half of the story in the college classroom.
Helping students understand and more efficiently use their
learning strategies recognizes the importance of this other half
of the equation.*

Assessing and Improving Students' Learning Strategies

Paul R. Pintrich, Glenn Ross Johnson

College students engage in a variety of learning activities in different
classrooms. They attend lectures, engage in discussions and small group
collaborations, perform laboratory exercises, work problems, read textbook and primary sources, and study for exams. Performing these activities adequately requires a variety of strategies. Some students seem to
develop appropriate learning strategies without much formal instruction;
others are limited in their repertoires and tend to rely on strategies that
are not necessarily appropriate for all learning activities (for example,
using rote rehearsal to study for an essay exam). Some students may
actually be knowledgeable about different strategies but are not motivated
to use them in different college courses (Pintrich, 1989). These two problems—lack of knowledge about appropriate learning strategies and lack
of motivation to use them—plague many college students and hinder
their learning.

Although there are many books and formal instructional programs
designed to help students improve their learning strategies, one key aspect
of most of the programs is the attempt to make them more aware of their
own cognition and motivation (for example, Brown, Bransford, Ferrara,
and Campione, 1983; Flavell, 1979; McKeachie, Pintrich, Lin, and Smith,
1986). The purpose of this chapter is to describe several assessment instruments that faculty can use to help students become more aware of their
own strategies and motivation for learning. Besides helping students
become more aware, the information generated by these instruments can
enlighten faculty members about the general cognitive and motivational

New Directions for Teaching and Learning, no. 42, Summer 1990 © Jossey-Bass Inc., Publishers characteristics of their students. This information, in turn, can be used in course planning and teaching.

Learning Styles and Learning Strategies

Many different theoretical views of student learning and motivation and a wide variety of assessment instruments are available. In this chapter we focus specifically on the literature on college student learning characterized by the terms *learning styles* and *learning strategies*. Although similar in some respects, these two literatures make different assumptions about learning and about students that have implications for the development of assessment instruments and for instruction.

Learning Styles. The learning styles literature (see Claxton and Murrell, 1987, for a review) is based on the assumption that individuals can be described by certain psychological characteristics, traits, or styles that influence the way they perceive, organize, and react to different environmental stimuli. Moreover, much of the research in this tradition assumes that these traits or styles are relatively stable across different situations and are not really under the learner's intentional control (Pintrich, forthcoming). For example, the Jungian-derived Myers-Briggs typology (Myers and McCauley, 1985) assumes that students can be categorized along four dimensions (extroverted-introverted, sensing-intuitive, thinking-feeling, and judging-perceptive) and that these preferences for interacting with information and other people are related to how students learn in all courses all the time.

One problem with the Myers-Briggs typology is that it is based on a general personality model that may not be closely related to the cognitive activities that most students are asked to perform in college classrooms. In contrast, Kolb (1984, 1985) has proposed an information-processing model of learning styles that is more related to the cognitive activities required in college classrooms. He suggests that there are four basic modes of information processing (concrete experience, reflective observation, abstract conceptualization, and active experimentation), which characterize how students tend to learn. These modes influence *what* students learn as well as *how* they adapt to the class. For example, a student who prefers concrete examples based on experience may have difficulty learning in a philosophy course that always focuses on abstract concepts.

In assuming stability as well as lack of individual control, these learning style models suggest that it may be difficult for students to change their learning styles. To combat this resistance, they propose that it may at least be helpful to make students aware of their learning styles, not because they can change them but rather because they can then try to adapt their behavior to match the demands of the courses or careers they choose to pursue. Another implication of these models is that faculty should attempt to adjust or adapt their course and teaching style to meet the learning style needs of the students enrolled in their courses (Claxton and Murrell, 1987).

Learning Strategies. Although the general idea of adapting instruction to individual differences is important in education (compare Corno and Snow, 1986), it may be difficult for many faculty members to change their teaching styles when limited by external constraints such as class size. In addition, current research in cognitive, social, and personality psychology suggests that the assumptions about stability and lack of control inherent in the traditional learning style approach may not be tenable (Cantor and Kihlstrom, 1987; Pintrich, forthcoming). Current research on student learning suggests that use of learning strategies can vary in different situations and that these strategies can be brought under the control of the student (McKeachie and others, 1986). For example, students may choose to study differently for a simple factual recall test in comparison to a test that requires application and transfer of the course material. In addition, recent research on student motivation and personality (Cantor and Kihlstrom, 1987; McKeachie and others, 1986) suggests that the strong-trait models proposed by many learning style models are not accurate and that motivational orientation also can vary in different situations and significantly affect learning.

Accordingly, the learning strategy approach emphasizes (1) the changeable nature of strategies and motivation due to situational demands and (2) the assumption that the use of different learning strategies can be controlled by the learner. Besides being based on more sophisticated theories and current research, the assumptions of the learning strategy approach hold out the promise to students that they can control and change their learning. In the same way, this approach suggests that faculty can take a more active and direct role in helping students improve their learning.

Learning Strategies in the College Classroom

There are many different models of learning strategies appropriate to the college level (see McKeachie and others, 1986, for a review), but two programs of research have generated assessment instruments that can be useful for general program planning and evaluation as well as for feedback to students and faculty. Both programs of research are based on general cognitive models of the student as an information processor.

As information processors, students must first be able to select what is important from lectures, discussions, and course reading. Then students must be able to understand how this new information can be integrated and connected to their previously acquired knowledge. Finally, students have to be able to remember the information in order for it to be used in new situations (for example, on a test or in a paper or lab report). This overly simple description does not capture the complexity of how students learn, remember, and understand (see McKeachie and others, 1986; Weinstein and Mayer, 1986, for more comprehensive descriptions), but it provides a useful framework for describing in more detail the two programs of research and their respective assessment instruments.

The Learning and Study Strategies Inventory (LASSI). Claire Weinstein and her colleagues at the Cognitive Strategies Project at the University of Texas, Austin, have developed a comprehensive model of learning strategies and an excellent instrument, the LASSI, to assess students' learning strategies (see Weinstein, Schulte, and Palmer, 1987; Weinstein, Zimmerman, and Palmer, 1988). The LASSI is a self-report questionnaire with seventy-seven items that takes approximately fifteen to twenty minutes to administer and can be self-scored by the student for immediate feedback. The validity and reliability data are very good for a self-report instrument and there are norms available for the different scales to assist in interpretation.

There are ten scales in the LASSI, five dealing with motivation and self-management and five with cognitive strategies. The motivation scales (attitude, motivation, and anxiety) reflect traditional definitions of motivation. The attitude scale taps students' general interests and goals for college. The motivation scale concerns students' willingness to accept responsibility for their school work and to put forth consistent effort. Students who score high on these scales should be more likely to use appropriate learning strategies. The anxiety scale reflects how much the student worries about exams and doing well on them. In contrast to the other two motivation scales, a high score on this scale is not conducive to good study habits. The next two self-management scales (time management and concentration) reflect students' skills at directing and controlling their study behavior. Time management concerns students' abilities to schedule their time and study in appropriate ways. Concentration involves students' strategies for focusing their attention on school tasks and avoiding distractions.

The cognitive scales (information processing, selecting main ideas, study aids, self-testing, and test strategies) are based on the general information-processing idea (for example, Weinstein and Mayer, 1986) that the more students become actively involved in trying to integrate and connect course material with their prior knowledge, the more likely they will be able to understand and learn the material. Accordingly, learning strategies that are more passive (for example, rehearsing, copying notes, underlining) are less likely to be beneficial for meaningful learning. The information-processing scale measures students' use of learning strategies such as paraphrasing and summarizing that should result in deeper, more elaborated learning. The selecting main ideas scale assesses students' skills at picking out the most important information to learn from lecturers and readings. The study aids scale measures the extent to which students use aids such as italics and headings, diagrams and charts, and group review sessions. The self-testing scale concerns students' use of strategies to review and check their understanding of course material. Finally, the test strategies scale evaluates students' use of effective test-taking strategies. On all five cognitive scales, students who use more of the strategies should be more effective learners (Weinstein, Zimmerman, and Palmer, 1988).

The Motivated Strategies for Learning Questionnaire (MSLQ). The MSLQ has been developed by a team of researchers at the Program on Learning and Teaching at the federally funded National Center for Research to Improve Postsecondary Teaching and Learning at the University of Michigan. The team has been co-directed by William McKeachie and Paul Pintrich. The MSLQ has been developed under the leadership of Pintrich (see Pintrich, 1988a, 1988b, 1989; Pintrich, McKeachie, and Smith, 1989).

The MSLQ, like the LASSI, is a self-report questionnaire that takes about twenty to thirty minutes to administer. The MSLQ has not been under development as long as the LASSI, but the reliability and validity data appear to be adequate (Pintrich, McKeachie, and Smith, 1989). The MSLQ is based on the same general information-processing model as the LASSI, but there are several differences. First, the motivational scales are based on a general social-cognitive approach to motivation that includes three general components: values, expectancy, and affect (Pintrich, 1988a). In addition, the MSLQ organizes its cognitive scales into general cognitive strategies and metacognitive strategies (executive processes that plan and direct learning). Finally, the last general category of scales on the MSLQ includes resource management factors (Pintrich, 1988a).

The motivation scales on the MSLQ include three value scales, two expectancy scales, and one affective scale. The intrinsic goal-orientation scale measures students' approaches to learning in terms of the adoption of goals of mastering and learning the course content. The extrinsic goal-orientation scale concerns students' orientations to course work in terms of the focus on some external reward (for example, to receive a high grade, to pass the course, to meet requirements). The final value scale, task value, assesses students' beliefs that the course material is useful, valuable, and interesting. Students who score high on all three of these value scales tend to use more cognitive strategies than students with lower scores (Pintrich, McKeachie, and Smith, 1989).

The expectancy scales include control beliefs, self-efficacy, and expectancy for success. The control beliefs scale measures the extent to which students believe they can control their learning and use cognitive strategies in comparison to the belief that they cannot control their own learning. The self-efficacy scale reflects students' self-confidence that they can learn and master the course content. The expectancy for success scale concerns students' beliefs that they will do well in the course. Higher scores on these three scales are correlated with more cognitive engagement and better performance (Pintrich, McKeachie, and Smith, 1989). The affective scale, test anxiety, concerns students' worries and anxieties in testing situations. In comparison to the three expectancy scales, the higher the score on the test anxiety scale, the less likely the students are to do well in the course.

The cognitive and metacognitive scales on the MSLQ reflect a basic information-processing model (McKeachie and others, 1986). The rehearsal scale assesses students' use of basic strategies for recalling information such as repeating important information or recopying notes. Although rehearsal strategies may not result in deeper processing of course information, in some courses with much material to be memorized, they seem to be effective (see Pintrich, 1989; Pintrich, McKeachie, and Smith, 1989). The elaboration scale reflects students' use of summarizing and paraphrasing strategies. The organization scale measures students' use of strategies to outline, integrate, and connect information. The metacognition scale concerns students' use of planning, monitoring, and regulating strategies. For example, students who attempt to set goals for themselves when studying demonstrate planning behavior. Monitoring behavior includes checking for self-comprehension of lectures and readings. Regulating behaviors include going back and reviewing or restudying class notes or readings to improve comprehension. Finally, the critical thinking scale reflects students' attempts at analyzing or questioning the assumptions inherent in the course material. Students who engage in all of these five types of strategies should learn more in their courses than students who use few of the strategies (Pintrich, McKeachie, and Smith, 1989).

The final category of scales on the MSLQ concerns how students manage themselves, their time, their study environments, and others. The time and study management scale reflects students' organization of their study schedules and study environments. The effort management scale assesses students' regulation of their efforts and willingness to persist in the face of difficulties. The help-seeking behavior scale concerns students' use of peers and teachers for assistance in studying and learning. Students who manage their resources carefully, especially their own efforts, tend to perform better than students who are not good managers (Pintrich, McKeachie, and Smith, 1989).

Implications for Learners and Teachers

For learners, both the LASSI and the MSLQ can serve to increase awareness of the use of different learning strategies as well as the motivation for using them. By providing feedback to students on their relative levels of motivation and cognition, the data from the LASSI and the MSLQ can motivate students to seek formal or informal help to improve their learning. We have found that many students are not aware of the possibility of different learning strategies, so that even taking the MSLQ or the LASSI can be beneficial. Of course, the feedback from these instruments can be used in a diagnostic manner to identify areas of motivation or learning strategies that need improvement (Pintrich, McKeachie, and Smith, 1989; Weinstein, Zimmerman, and Palmer, 1988).

For teachers, the class aggregate information from these two instruments provides a "snapshot" of the motivational and cognitive level of the class as a whole. This type of feedback can be very useful to faculty members since it describes in detail and complexity the nature of their students. This type of descriptive information on the class can be much richer than the simple descriptions many faculty members might normally generate in the course of a semester (for example, "They do not learn because they are too stupid" and "They are not interested") and therefore can be more useful in identifying effective strategies to overcome deficits.

In addition, if faculty fill out the MSLQ or the LASSI in terms of their "ideal student" and then compare their ideals to the actual data from their classes, discrepancies may generate some ideas about different ways to teach. The descriptive information on the different scales can then provide a path of communication not only between faculty and students but also between faculty and faculty-development specialists about student learning. The information provides a concrete and specific language for a discussion of how students learn and how they are motivated.

Both the instruments and the models they are based on assume that students' motivation and use of learning strategies can be changed through teaching. This provides faculty with the opportunity to actually try to improve students' motivation and cognition. Cross and Angelo (1988) and Johnson and others (1989) have provided some excellent suggestions for users of either the LASSI or the MSLQ. What follows are some suggestions that derive from consideration of the various components of the models on which these instruments are based. The suggestions illustrate how information from these instruments can be used to fine-tune teaching.

Student Motivation Interventions. When students score low (1) on *intrinsic motivation,* have them contrast their own ideas and thoughts with those discussed in the text materials and by the instructor, thus tying course material to already existing sources of motivation; (2) on *task value,* have them analyze the course syllabus and suggest to them how the course will provide for their future needs, or use in-class time to discuss how they might benefit from taking the course; (3) on *self-efficacy,* schedule conferences with individual students and provide helpful feedback; and (4) on *expectancy for success,* require the students to describe how they learn and provide feedback on how their learning methods can best be used in the course.

When students score high on *student anxiety,* avoid tests and other assignments that exacerbate the problem. One of the easiest ways to do this, for example, is to remove strict time limits for exams. Unless the instructor is interested in testing students' swiftness in completing the task, relaxed time limits allow the test results to reflect ability to perform the task, unhampered by test anxiety.

Cognitive Strategies Interventions. The assessment instruments also help pinpoint the use of ineffective strategies that need revision. Faculty members can actually teach students how to use the different learning strategies in the context of their own specific classes by modeling their own thinking and requiring students to practice in class. For example, if students tend to use rehearsal strategies when more sophisticated strategies are called for, the instructor can provide opportunities for (1) *elaboration:* at the end of the lecture, have the students summarize the main idea in one paragraph and turn the summary in; (2) *organization:* have students prepare an outline of each reading to use as a study guide; (3) *metacognition:* have students submit possible exam questions and answers at the end of the lecture; and (4) *critical thinking:* have students discuss and agree on one assumption underlying some assertion in the reading.

Resource Management Interventions. Perhaps the most difficult task for and most frequent shortcoming of students is resource management. Once the instruments have highlighted potential problem areas, the instructor could discuss the important aspects of setting realistic study times, establishing and sticking to study schedules, attending classes, completing reading assignments, and reviewing notes. Having students complete work logs or schedule projects across the span of the semester can introduce students to the concept of paced work.

These are just a few examples of the kinds of interventions that faculty could devise to help students become more effective learners once they have identified their learning strategies through use of instruments like the LASSI and the MSLQ. Despite all this research and development work, however, it is important that faculty continue to try different teaching strategies and adapt these strategies to their courses, their students, and the local contexts. There is no one panacea or "magic bullet" to improve learning and motivation. It is only through the thoughtful adaptation of these ideas, models, and instruments to the individual faculty member's situation that we can improve students' learning of course content and about learning itself.

References

Brown, A. L., Bransford, J. D., Ferrara, R. A., and Campione, J. C. "Learning, Remembering, and Understanding." In P. H. Mussen (ed.), *Handbook of Child Psychology*. Vol. 3. New York: Wiley, 1983.

Cantor, N., and Kihlstrom, J. *Personality and Social Intelligence*. Englewood Cliffs, N.J.: Prentice Hall, 1987.

Claxton, C. S., and Murrell, P. H. *Learning Styles: Implications for Improving Educational Practices*. ASHE-ERIC Higher Education Reports, no. 4. Washington, D.C.: Association for the Study of Higher Education, 1987.

Corno, L., and Snow, R. E. "Adapting Teaching to Individual Differences Among Learners." In M. C. Wittrock (ed.), *Handbook of Research on Teaching*. New York: Macmillan, 1986.

Cross, K. P., and Angelo, T. A. *Classroom Assessment Techniques: A Handbook for Faculty*. Ann Arbor: National Center for Research to Improve Postsecondary Teaching and Learning, University of Michigan, 1988.

Flavell, J. H. "Metacognition and Cognitive Monitoring: A New Area of Cognitive-Developmental Inquiry." *American Psychologist*, 1979, *34*, 906–911.

Johnson, G. R., Eison, J. A., Abbott, R., Meiss, G. T., Moran, J. A., Pasternack, T. L., and Zaremba, E. *Teaching Tips for Users of the Motivated Strategies for Learning Questionnaire (MSLQ)*. Ann Arbor: National Center for Research to Improve Postsecondary Teaching and Learning, University of Michigan, 1989.

Kolb, D. A. *Experiential Learning: Experience as the Source of Learning and Development*. New York: Prentice Hall, 1984.

Kolb, D. A. *The Learning-Style Inventory*. Boston: McBer, 1985.

McKeachie, W. J., Pintrich, P. R., Lin, Y. G., and Smith, D. *Teaching and Learning in the College Classroom: A Review of the Research Literature*. Ann Arbor: National Center for Research to Improve Postsecondary Teaching and Learning, University of Michigan, 1986.

Myers, I. B., and McCauley, M. H. *The Myers-Briggs Manual: A Guide to the Development and Use of the Myers-Briggs Type Indicator*. Palo Alto, Calif.: Consulting Psychologists Press, 1985.

Pintrich, P. R. "A Process-Oriented View of Student Motivation and Cognition." In J. S. Stark and L. A. Mets (eds.), *Improving Teaching and Learning Through Research*. New Directions for Institutional Research, no. 57. San Francisco: Jossey-Bass, 1988a.

Pintrich, P. R. "Student Learning and College Teaching." In R. E. Young and K. E. Eble (eds.), *College Teaching and Learning: Preparing for New Commitments*. New Directions for Teaching and Learning, no. 33. San Francisco: Jossey-Bass, 1988b.

Pintrich, P. R. "The Dynamic Interplay of Student Motivation and Cognition in the College Classroom." In C. Ames and M. Maehr (eds.), *Advances in Motivation and Achievement: Motivation Enhancing Environments*. Vol. 6. Greenwich, Conn.: JAI Press, 1989.

Pintrich, P. R. "Implications of the Psychological Research on College Learning and Teaching for Teacher Education." In R. Houston (ed.), *The Handbook of Research on Teacher Education*. New York: Macmillan, in press.

Pintrich, P. R., McKeachie, W. J., and Smith, D. *The Motivated Strategies for Learning Questionnaire*. Ann Arbor: National Center for Research to Improve Postsecondary Teaching and Learning, University of Michigan, 1989.

Weinstein, C. E., and Mayer, R. "The Teaching of Learning Strategies." In

M. Wittrock (ed.), *Handbook of Research on Teaching*. New York: Macmillan, 1986.

Weinstein, C. E., Schulte, A. C., and Palmer, D. R. *Learning and Study Strategies Inventory (LASSI)*. Clearwater, Fla.: H. and H. Publishing, 1987.

Weinstein, C. E., Zimmerman, S. A., and Palmer, D. R. "Assessing Learning Strategies: The Design and Development of the LASSI." In C. E. Weinstein, E. T. Goetz, and P. A. Alexander (eds.), *Learning and Study Strategies*. San Diego, Calif.: Academic Press, 1988.

Paul R. Pintrich is assistant professor of psychology and co-director of the Program on Teaching and Learning at the University of Michigan, Ann Arbor.

Glenn Ross Johnson is professor of curriculum and instruction and director of the Center for Teaching Excellence at Texas A&M University, College Station.

Understanding how students and faculty are alike and different
in their attitudes toward learning and grading can provide
some guidance in organizing courses to meet the diverse
motivations of both groups.

Grades: Their Influence on Students and Faculty

Fred Janzow, James Eison

In 1783, faculty at Yale University assigned one of four grades to students: Optime (Honor Men), Second Optime (Pass Men), Inferiores (Charity Passes), and Pejores (Unmentionables) (Milton, Pollio, and Eison, 1986). Since that time, grades have become an ever-increasing source of exasperation for both students and faculty; grades have also been the subject of considerable professional writing but significantly less scholarly research. The present chapter *will not* (1) provide an extensive historical review of grading practices (see Cureton, 1971; Smallwood, 1935), (2) offer a detailed indictment of current grading practices (see Kirchbaum, Simon, and Napier, 1971; Milton, Pollio, and Eison, 1986), or (3) attempt to defend various grading practices (see Ebel, 1980; McKeachie, 1976). Rather, this chapter examines critically the impact that different orientations toward grades and toward learning have on students and faculty and the importance of understanding each orientation. The discussion also suggests a means by which faculty can assess these orientations to enhance the teaching/learning process.

Students' Views About Learning and Grading

In a recent article Benjamin DeMott (1988, p. 54) asked, "Is not knowing *whom* you're talking to as bad as not knowing *what* you're talking about [emphasis added]?" With respect to understanding the impact grades have on students, we assume that a faculty member's own undergraduate experiences often produce a false picture of how today's students think, feel, and act. For example, a national survey (Milton, Pollio, and Eison,

1986) of over 850 faculty from twenty-three campuses revealed that 61 percent made "mostly A's" in college; only 23 percent of over 4,350 undergraduates on these campuses reported making "mostly A's." Thus, faculty members are not like most students in that we have been the victors rather than the victims of various grading systems; and our love of learning has led us to choose careers in academe rather than the prewealth career options the majority of today's undergraduates pursue. This difference between faculty and student experiences highlights the need for faculty to obtain data about their students.

In this pursuit, Eison (1981) and later Eison, Pollio, and Milton (1982) postulated the presence of two different student orientations at work in the classroom: (1) a learning orientation (LO), described as attitudes and behaviors based on the view that college courses provide an opportunity to acquire knowledge and obtain personal enlightenment and (2) a grade orientation (GO), described as attitudes and behaviors based on the view that the pursuit of course grades is a sufficient reason for being, and doing, in college. A self-report inventory, known as LOGO II, was created to assess these two student orientations; eight sample items from LOGO II appear in Table 1.

A two-dimensional model describing four types of students was proposed: high LO/high GO, high LO/low GO, low LO/high GO, low LO/low GO. Empirically determined descriptions of these four student groups were produced using the Sixteen Personality Factor Questionnaire (Cattell, Eber, and Tatusuoka, 1974), the Survey of Study Habits and Attitudes (Brown and Holtzman, 1967), the Achievement Anxiety Test

Table 1. Sample Items from LOGO II

Learning-Oriented Attitudes	I find the process of learning new material fun. A teacher's comments on an essay test mean more to me than my actual test score.
Learning-Oriented Behaviors	I stay after interesting classes to discuss material with the instructors. I do optional reading that my instructors suggest even though I know it won't affect my grade.
Grade-Oriented Attitudes	I think grades provide me a good goal to work toward. I dislike courses that require ungraded out-of-class activities.
Grade-Oriented Behaviors	When looking at a syllabus on the first day of class, I turn to the section on tests and grades first. I cut classes when confident that lecture material will not be on the exam.

Source: Adapted from Eison, 1981; and Eison, Pollio, and Milton, 1982.

(Alpert and Haber, 1960), the Levenson Internal, Powerful Other, and Chance scales (Levenson, 1981), and the Myers-Briggs Type Indicator (MBTI) (Myers, 1962). The four groups are summarized in Table 2 (Eison, Pollio, and Milton, 1986; Rogers and Palmer, 1987).

What Do Students Really Think?

LOGO II data (Eison and Pollio, 1989) obtained from over five thousand undergraduates enrolled in one large research university, four regional state universities, one liberal arts college, and two community colleges provide faculty with one helpful way of "knowing whom you're talking to." For example, from a low of 86 percent to a high of 92 percent of

Table 2. Descriptions of Students in the Four LOGO II Groups

	Low Grade-Orientation	High Grade-Orientation
High Learning-Orientation	*(High LO/Low GO)* Highest level of abstract reasoning Most sensitive Most self-motivated and inner-directed Greatest interest in new ideas and intellectual matters Lowest levels of tension and frustration Most intuitive Strongest internal locus-of-control Least conviction in luck or fate Best study habits and attitudes Greatest facilitating test anxiety Least debilitating text anxiety Most likely to have won honor society or awards in high school Most likely to read newspapers and books on a regular basis	*(High LO/High GO)* Lowest level of abstract reasoning Very tough minded and realistic Most extroverted Greatest believers in luck or fate Highest levels of debilitating test anxiety
Low Learning-Orientation	*(Low LO/Low GO)* Highest level of tension and frustration Most introverted	*(Low LO/High GO)* Most practical and conventional Very tough minded and realistic Most conservative and respecting of traditional ideas High levels of tension and anxiety Highest scores on "sensing" scale of MBTI (least intuitive) Lowest levels of internal locus-of-control Least facilitating test anxiety Poorest study habits and attitudes

Source: Adapted from Eison, Pollio, and Milton, 1986.

students across the institutions sampled agreed or agreed strongly with the statement, "I enjoy classes in which the instructor attempts to relate material to concerns beyond the classroom," and 28 percent to 57 percent reported that they "get annoyed when lectures or class presentations are only rehashes of easy reading assignments." Faculty, therefore, are well advised to explicitly incorporate course material into the larger framework of students' lives, and to interpret, rather than restate, textbook material during lectures.

With respect to attitudes toward tests, 44 percent to 59 percent said "without regularly scheduled exams, I would not learn and remember very much"; but 23 percent to 34 percent "prefer to write a term paper on interesting material than to take a test on the same general topic." While 50 percent of the students reported that tests are needed to motivate their learning, approximately 33 percent reported a preference for alternative forms of evaluation (for example, writing a term paper). One obvious implication of these two results is that we need to provide opportunities for students to choose between frequent tests or other learning activities.

While 87 percent to 91 percent of the students reported that they "appreciate the instructor who provides honest and detailed evaluation of my work, though such evaluation is sometimes unpleasant," 25 percent to 38 percent reported that "written assignments (for example, homework and projects) that are not graded are a waste of a student's time." It is clear that most students desire detailed feedback about their work and that some students view ungraded written assignments with disdain.

Since publication of LOGO II, a number of studies have examined the relationships between other student characteristics and orientations toward learning and grades. These studies have provided the following, instructionally helpful results:

1. During standard fifty-minute lectures, high GO students are more likely than high LO students to look attentive when their thoughts are not focused on the lecture (Pollio, 1984). Rather than rely strictly on nonverbal cues to assess students' attention during lectures, faculty may want to interrupt their lectures at appropriate times and ask students to write short summaries of what they have learned. A brief assessment of these summaries would permit the instructor to determine the degree to which students have clearly understood the presentation.

2. High GO students worry more than high LO students about personal relationships, career, money, and school (McDaniel and Eison, 1986). Although most faculty have few opportunities to deal directly with students' worries, they can look for warning signs that excessive worry is impeding the academic performance of high GO students and refer these students to campus counseling centers.

3. Students in various academic majors differ in their LO and GO scores (for example, business majors tended to be low LO/high GO,

social science majors tended to be high LO/high GO, and humanities majors tended to be high LO/low GO) (Rogers and Palmer, 1987; Rogers, Palmer, and Bolen, 1988). Within their particular disciplines, faculty might wish to create classroom environments that meet the LO or GO preferences of their students. Furthermore, they might wish to discuss with students the importance of developing abilities to learn successfully in both learning-oriented and grade-oriented classroom situations. Additionally, faculty should consider how their personal orientations to grades and learning conflict with, or complement, their students' orientations.

4. Students who participated in honors programs were significantly more learning-oriented than grade-oriented (Henry and Adams, 1988; Stephens and Eison, 1986–1987). These findings suggest that instructors of honors classes can use learning-oriented strategies (for example, ungraded work, alternative assignments, interdisciplinary readings) to enhance student learning.

5. Students with low SAT scores were reported to be more grade-oriented than learning-oriented (Johnson and Beck, 1989). This finding suggests that in classes consisting predominantly of students with low SAT scores, regularly scheduled examinations and conventionally graded assignments can be used to motivate students to study.

6. Seniors reported significantly higher LO scores and significantly lower GO scores than freshmen (Rogers, Palmer, and Bolen, 1988). At one liberal arts college in Alabama (University of Montevallo) students appeared to develop greater learning orientations as they progressed through the academic program. If this finding can be generalized to other institutions, it suggests that faculty who teach upper-division courses are well advised to use different teaching strategies from those employed in lower-division courses.

Although many faculty members view their students as a relatively homogeneous group (and teach accordingly), these findings clearly demonstrate that motivational diversity exists in every classroom. Faculty members should consider these differences when planning course activities and assignments. Readers interested in learning more about the LOGO II inventory should contact James Eison, the co-author of this chapter.

Faculty Views About Learning and Grades

A natural extension of the LOGO II research explored the question, "To what degree do faculty members differ in their views about learning and grades?" To address this question, a faculty questionnaire, known as LOGO F, was developed following the model and procedures used to develop LOGO II. Pilot testing of forty-eight items produced twenty statements, which measured the following four dimensions: learning-oriented attitudes, learning-oriented behaviors, grade-oriented attitudes, and grade-oriented behaviors. Table 3 contains eight sample items from LOGO F.

What Do Faculty Really Think?

LOGO F data have been collected from over thirteen hundred faculty employed at three regional state universities, two liberal arts colleges, and two community colleges (Eison, Janzow, and Pollio, 1989). Factor analysis of the twenty items revealed that learning orientation in faculty is characterized by (1) the belief that grades are overvalued (for example, "I think my colleagues across campus place too much emphasis on using grades to motivate students"); (2) instructor flexibility (for example, "I am willing to make exceptions to stated graded criteria when unusual circumstances arise"); and (3) a preference for collaboration over competition (for example, "I think students should be encouraged to collaborate rather than compete").

Grade orientation in faculty is characterized by (1) teaching to the best and the brightest (for example, "I set grading standards that are designed primarily to challenge the brightest students in my classes"); (2) being concerned about grade inflation (for example, "I worry about colleagues who are giving an ever increasing number of A's and B's");

Table 3. Sample Items from LOGO F

Learning-Oriented Attitudes	Students' concern about grades often interferes with learning in my classroom.
	I would prefer teaching a course in which no grades were given than a typical graded course.
Learning-Oriented Behaviors	I encourage students to raise questions in class that are topic-related but which go beyond the scope of the tests that I prepare.
	I design course assignments that encourage students to read outside of my discipline.
Grade-Oriented Attitudes	Without regularly scheduled exams most students would not learn the material I present.
	I wish my colleagues across the campus were tougher graders.
Grade-Oriented Behaviors	I orient my teaching style (for example, content, pace, difficulty level) to satisfy the needs of upper-level students (and hope that the others can keep up).
	I encourage students to focus primarily on their studies and to limit their participation in extracurricular activities that might jeopardize their GPA.

Source: Adapted from Eison, Janzow, and Pollio, 1989.

(3) focusing students toward the significance of grades (for example, "I emphasize in my conversations with students the importance of studying to obtain 'good grades' "; and (4) believing that grades are useful and informative (for example, "I reward student improvement and growth by weighing the students' progress in my grading system").

An instructor's orientation toward grades and learning can have important implications for teaching. Faculty who mistakenly assume that all or most students share their educational values may create an educational environment that better serves the instructor than the students.

While LOGO F responses obtained on seven campuses revealed a surprising degree of inter-institutional similarity, considerable intra-institutional diversity among faculty members was noted. Across these institutions, between 55 percent and 70 percent of the faculty agreed or agreed strongly with the statement, "Without regularly scheduled exams, most students would not learn the material I present," while 20 percent to 30 percent disagreed or disagreed strongly with this item. Similarly, 25 percent to 40 percent of the faculty agreed or agreed strongly with the statement, "I think college grades are good predictors of success in later life," while 25 percent to 35 percent disagreed or disagreed strongly with this statement. Given this diversity of views, heated discussion among faculty inevitably occurs whenever changes in campus grading policies or practices are proposed.

The Interaction Between Faculties' and Students' Views

Though the development of student orientation toward grades probably results from many interrelated influences, the grade-oriented attitudes and behaviors of some faculty are surely of significance in shaping students' views. For example, 60 percent to 65 percent of the faculty agreed or agreed strongly with the statement, "I think it useful to use grades as incentives to increase student performance," and 20 percent to 30 percent reported often or always emphasizing in conversations with students the importance of studying to obtain "good grades." These responses make it easy to understand why many students exhibit a stronger orientation toward grades than toward learning. The behavior of faculty, and the impact of academic reward systems, reinforce the value students place on grades—often in the absence of faculty introspection about the influence grades have on the teaching-learning process.

Recommendations

These studies provide readers with an opportunity for thinking about the impact faculty and student orientations have on teaching and learning. With this in mind, five recommendations are offered:

1. Adjusting Socrates' sage advice, we urge faculty and students to "know thine selves." Faculty and students can benefit from personal reflection on their orientations toward grades and toward learning. Readers are encouraged to use LOGO II and LOGO F as one way of promoting self-awareness. For example, at the start of a semester instructors could complete LOGO F and students could complete LOGO II. Faculty might then use the student data to stimulate class discussion and use the LOGO F data to help guide their choice of teaching strategies.

2. Given that most classes are composed of heterogeneous groups of students, faculty are encouraged to include in their courses some activities specifically directed toward high LO students (for example, relating course material to concerns beyond the classroom and not rehashing easy reading assignments during lectures), and other activities directed toward high GO students (for example, ensuring that exams cover lecture material and grading all written assignments). The same is true for evaluation methods; overdependence on true-false and multiple-choice exams might favor GO students. A singular emphasis on grade-oriented activities and assignments runs the risk of reducing the motivation of high LO students, while an overemphasis on ungraded work may do the same for high GO students.

3. Realizing that students need to learn to operate effectively in both LO and GO environments, faculty should explicitly discuss this issue in their classes when course syllabi are distributed, when class tests are returned, and when final course grades are assigned. These are particularly appropriate times to discuss those student attitudes and behaviors related most to academic success.

4. One function of grades is to reinforce student behaviors that faculty members consider most important. Thus, faculty members should weigh carefully how the grades they assign reward desired behaviors. For example, if creativity is viewed as important, the grading scheme should explicitly reward creative thoughts and acts. Or, if a faculty member hopes to stimulate independent thought and self-directed learning, these too should be prominent components of a student's grade.

5. Readers are encouraged to use LOGO II and LOGO F in classroom research projects, as described in a previous chapter by Angelo. Faculty can use these two instruments to obtain a better understanding of the association between these orientations and students' reactions to various types of course assignments, instructor behaviors, and grading practices.

Conclusion

Few instructional practices exert greater influence on teaching and learning in the classroom than a faculty member's grading practices. It is our belief that open-minded reflection, data collection, and critical thinking in relation to the impact of grades on learning are as basic to effective teaching as the same three activities are in relation to scholarly research in one's discipline. As readers contemplate the changing face of college teaching, the impact of grades on students and faculty should be considered carefully, both institutionally and personally.

References

Alpert, R., and Haber, R. "Anxiety in Academic Achievement Situations." *Journal of Abnormal and Social Psychology*, 1960, *61*, 207-215.

Brown, W., and Holtzman, W. *The Survey of Study Habits and Attitudes Manual.* New York: Psychological Corporation, 1967.

Cattell, R., Eber, H., and Tatusuoka, M. *Handbook for the Sixteen Personality Factor Questionnaire.* Champaign, Ill.: Institute for Personality and Ability Testing, 1974.

Cureton, L. W. "The History of Grading Practices." *Measurement in Education*, 1971, *2* (4), 1-9.

DeMott, B. "Do We Teach Students or Subjects?" *Change*, 1988, *20* (1), 54.

Ebel, R. L. *Practical Problems in Educational Measurement.* Lexington, Mass.: D. C. Heath, 1980.

Eison, J. "A New Instrument for Assessing Students' Orientations Towards Grades and Learning." *Psychological Reports*, 1981, *48*, 919-924.

Eison, J., Janzow, F., and Pollio, H. R. *LOGO F: A User's Manual.* Cape Girardeau: Center for Teaching and Learning, Southeast Missouri State University, 1989.

Eison, J., and Pollio, H. R. *LOGO II: Bibliographic and Statistical Update.* (Rev. ed.). Cape Girardeau: Center for Teaching and Learning, Southeast Missouri State University, 1989.

Eison, J., Pollio, H. R., and Milton, O. *LOGO II: A User's Manual.* Knoxville: Learning Research Center, University of Tennessee, 1982.

Eison, J., Pollio, H. R., and Milton, O. "Educational and Personal Characteristics of Four Different Types of Learning- and Grade-Oriented Students." *Contemporary Educational Psychology*, 1986, *11*, 54-67.

Henry, S. M., and Adams, J. F. "Academic Achievers: Predicting Participation in Honors Programs." Paper presented at the Southeastern Psychological Association, New Orleans, La., March 1988.

Johnson, B. G., and Beck, H. P. "Strict and Lenient Grading Scales: How Do They Affect the Performance of College Students with High and Low SAT Scores?" *Teaching of Psychology*, 1989, *15* (3), 127-131.

Kirchbaum, H., Simon, S., and Napier, R. *Wad-ja-get?* New York: Hart, 1971.

Levenson, H. "Differentiating Among Internality, Powerful Others, and Chance." In H. Lefcourt (ed.), *Research with the Locus of Control Construct.* Vol. 1. New York: Academic Press, 1981.

McDaniel, P., and Eison, J. "The Relationship Between College Student Worries and Other Measures of Health and Adjustment." Unpublished manuscript, Southeast Missouri State University, 1986.

McKeachie, W. J. "College Grades: A Rationale and Mild Defense." *American Association of University Professors Bulletin*, 1976, *62*, 320-322.

Milton, O., Pollio, H. R., and Eison, J. *Making Sense of College Grades*. San Francisco: Jossey-Bass, 1986.

Myers, I. B. *The Myers-Briggs Type Indicator Manual*. Palo Alto, Calif.: Consulting Psychologists Press, 1962.

Pollio, H. R. "What Students Think About and Do in College Lecture Classes." In *Teaching-Learning Issues*, no. 53. Knoxville: University of Tennessee, 1984.

Rogers, J., and Palmer, W. R. "Learning and Grade Orientation Profile of a College Freshman Class." Paper presented at the annual meeting of the Mid-South Educational Research Association, Mobile, Ala., March 1987.

Rogers, J., Palmer, W. R., and Bolen, L. "In Pursuit of Lifelong Learning: A Comparison of Learning and Grade Orientation of Freshmen and Seniors." Paper presented at the annual meeting of the Southeastern Psychological Association, New Orleans, La., March 1988.

Smallwood, M. L. *A Historical Study of Examinations and Grading Systems in Early American Universities*. Cambridge, Mass.: Harvard University Press, 1935.

Stephens, J., and Eison, J. "A Comparative Investigation of Honors and Non-Honors Students." *Forum for Honors*, 1986-1987, *17* (1-2), 17-25.

Fred Janzow is an associate professor of biology at Southeast Missouri State University, Cape Girardeau.

James Eison is the director of the Center for Teaching and Learning at Southeast Missouri State University.

Efforts to enhance student motivation can be made more effective if they are approached from the perspective of psychological models of what drives human behavior.

Using Psychological Models to Understand Student Motivation

Ann F. Lucas

One of the most frequent questions asked by concerned faculty in higher education is "What can I do to motivate students?" Unfortunately, there are no easy answers to this question; but for professors who take teaching seriously, there is an extensive body of literature on theories of motivation. Not only can these conceptual models be applied in the classroom to guide practice, but they can also significantly affect the way we look at teaching and learning. Each model contributes a slightly different perspective on how motivation might be operating, and each suggests instructional possibilities. The purpose of this chapter is to explain a variety of the most important current theories, demonstrate how an instructor would view classroom behavior from each perspective, and suggest a few implications of each model for teaching.

Theory 1: Social Learning Theory

Tenet. Motivation is a result of experiencing success or failure, directly or through observation of others.

There are two aspects to social learning theory that inform our question of how to motivate students most directly. One is the idea of the influence of success or failure; the other is the idea of observational learning.

Traditional learning theory states that behavior that is rewarded is likely to increase in frequency, whereas behavior that is not rewarded or is punished is likely to decrease in frequency. Going beyond the basic behaviorist view that all behavior can thus be controlled externally, social learning theory places an emphasis on the central role played by thought processes in mediating the effects of environmental change (Bandura and Walters, 1963; Bandura, 1977a, 1977b). In this view, learning is not simply a matter of reacting to stimuli. Rather, people apply cognitive processes that give meaning to the situation they encounter and in this way construct reality, putting personal labels on situations, evaluating their own performance, and rewarding or punishing themselves.

Further, in social learning theory, a lot of behavior is acquired through observational learning, that is, by looking at the way other people do things and noting the consequences of their actions. In observational learning, other students as well as the instructor can serve as models, for both the behavior being learned and the consequences. For example, if another student responds to a question posed by a professor, and that response, though not perfect, is not criticized but accepted as a contribution to the topic, a more timid student may volunteer the next time, having vicariously learned that responses will be accepted and not punished.

Implications for Teaching: The Role of Reinforcement. What are the practical applications of social learning theory for the college classroom? Let us begin with the first time a class meets, which creates a climate for the rest of the semester. The way a professor structures that first class can evoke anxiety or let students know it is safe to take risks, to think out loud rather than to wait to participate until they have come to the final "correct answer." When an ambience is created during the first class in which students feel they are valued members of a learning community who will be sharing some excitement together, students come to expect an enjoyable class. The first class also provides an opportunity for the instructor to give early positive feedback, which is a powerful force in shaping the subsequent behavior of students. Although all professors have had difficult students at one time or another, a positive climate created on that first day of class, and continued through the semester, can prevent hostile interactions because students learn they do not have to be on the defensive. When we are willing to listen attentively and summarize thoughts or emotions they have expressed, students know they are being taken seriously, which is rewarding. Moreover, social learning theorists tell us that attention is one of the most powerful reinforcers we can give to other individuals.

Educators are sometimes concerned about students who are seemingly motivated primarily to achieve good grades. We want them to be intrinsically motivated by love of learning, or by interest in the subject matter. However, reinforcing good work is not simply yielding to students' extrinsic motivation. Getting good grades may be the initial reason a student works hard; however, positive feedback can increase feelings of competence and self-esteem that then take on the force of intrinsic motivation. Receiving such feedback from the instructor also increases students' abilities to monitor their own progress because they learn to recognize the types of behavior that are being reinforced by others.

On the negative side, the use of punishment in education is of dubious value because, although it tells students that they are wrong, it does not provide constructive and concrete information about how to redirect their efforts in order to be successful. The possibility of punishment is used sometimes to motivate students, but it may actually have the opposite effect. For example, we can try to motivate students by creating anxiety, telling them during the first class-meeting all the ways in which their behavior can lead to poor grades. While such an approach will certainly increase anxiety, too much anxiety may have a paralyzing rather than a motivating effect. And since individuals tend to avoid situations that evoke anxiety, it could easily happen that both motivation and attendance will be poor in a course where anxiety levels have been raised.

The Role of Observation. A second significant implication of social learning theory is the idea of observation and vicarious learning. Students learn not only by answering questions and receiving feedback but also by watching others. Therefore, even in large classes, questions and problem-solving exercises serve a useful purpose. Answers and feedback to one student have an effect on all students in the class.

Observational learning can also work to decrease motivation. The instructor who asks questions and accepts only one right answer, showing verbal and nonverbal disapproval of responses that miss the target, will have an effect far broader than anticipated. Other students, identifying with the one who has just spoken up in class, then experience this disapproval vicariously and are less likely to speak voluntarily. Such incidents can sometimes trigger an adversarial relationship between professor and students, which can generate hostility. When students feel attacked, they are likely to become defensive or argumentative, or to retreat into sullen silence. They certainly will not be motivated to try again.

A second aspect of observational learning is the effect on the motivation of the instructors. How we come across in the classroom is also a significant factor because we are role models for our students. McKeachie (1974, p. 10) holds that "probably no one thing is more important in education than the teacher's enthusiasm and energy." College teachers generally love their disciplines. For a student to observe the "scholarly mind at work," to discover on a regular basis an educator's genuine excitement about a field, is a powerful motivator. It is often said that enthusiasm is contagious. In social learning terms, students experience our excitement and enthusiasm vicariously, model that enthusiasm, and are thus rewarded for learning.

Overall, social learning theory encourages the instructor to recognize the importance of reward and punishment, both direct and vicarious, in the development of motivation, as well as the fact that a lot of behavior and motivation can be developed through modeling.

Theory 2: Personal Growth as a Primary Goal in Learning

Tenet. Motivation is developed by creating an environment in which achievement of educational goals is congruent with personal and professional goals.

This theory argues that personal development, which sets the stage for a lifetime of growth, is the central, integrating goal of a college education. Therefore, the facilitation of personal growth, as we recognize and respond to the developmental needs of students, should provide a unifying theme for higher education.

What do we mean by personal growth and development? Ericksen (1984, p. 47) writes that students "have interests to nourish, values to examine, informational gaps to fill, and beliefs to strengthen." Cardinal Newman's ideas of a university, written in 1852, have been restated by Chickering and others (1981, p. 3) in their following list of values and objectives for education: "intellectual competence, ego development, moral and ethical development, humanitarian concern, interpersonal competence, capacity for intimacy, and vocational development."

Intellectual competence has been defined by Newman (1973, p. 177) as the ability "to see things as they are, to go right to the point, to disentangle a skein of thought, to detect what is sophisticated and to discard what is irrelevant," which implies critical thinking skills, analysis, synthesis, and evaluation. Moral and ethical development, which is now (albeit belatedly) becoming an educational concern in medicine, law, and business, can be defined as having a clear view of one's own opinions and values, becoming conscious of standards one can use in developing them, and being able to express them clearly and forcefully. Interpersonal competence has been described as being able to seek and offer help, being willing and able to influence others, and creating a network of honest communication with others. A capacity for intimacy is characterized by a willingness and ability to commit oneself to close, caring relationships in adult friendship and love. Vocational development involves the acquisition of knowledge and skills necessary for a particular career.

Although many students view attendance at college as a way of completing their education so that they can secure good jobs, it is obvious that even professional or vocational development is not achieved once and for all at the end of formal schooling. Rather, it is an ongoing process throughout life as one becomes recertified, changes careers, and reevaluates satisfactions. Students who come to recognize how the goals of a college education relate to their own growth goals will then be motivated to work toward those ends more vigorously.

Implications for Teaching. As with social learning theory this model leads us to two important educational considerations. The first requires that the overall goals of the college and the specific goals of each course be examined for congruence with one another and with students' personal and professional goals. Success in motivating students is more likely when faculty agree on educational goals and are themselves committed to them. Students are likely to be more highly motivated when they can fully appreciate how the objectives of each course that they take will help them achieve both overall educational goals and their own personal and professional goals. College, then, is no longer a series of fragmented parts but rather a truly integrated experience.

Within a given course, individual topics are constantly related to the overall goals. Examinations are made more meaningful by tying them in with the stated goals of the course. Class discussions elicit frequent feedback from students about how the class is progressing toward the goals that have been set. Faculty might use poor performances on quizzes as problem-solving opportunities instead of feeling defensive about the way in which the papers were graded or treating them as grounds to criticize students.

Personal development of students, then, is viewed as the integrating theme to alleviate the fragmentation of the curriculum as faculty, pushed by institutional emphasis on research, become specialists in subdisciplines that are increasingly narrow. And the emphasis on that personal development in all the goals of the curriculum lays the groundwork for increasing motivation.

The second necessary component implied by this theory is that college goals must be clearly delineated so that all students are not only keenly aware of these educational objectives but also understand how the segments of their experience fit together to make a meaningful whole. Therefore, goals must not only be integrated across courses and departments but also be communicated to the students. And efforts must be made to help the students articulate the relationship between the stated goals of a course and their own personal and professional goals.

Theory 3: Cognitive Development Theory

Tenet. Motivation requires a match between educational goals and the style of learning or stage of development of the learner.

Unless we have some understanding about how students learn, we are hampered in our attempts to teach them. It is obvious that we could never teach people to play tennis if we talked to them about the rudiments of the game but did not give them supervised practice time or feedback about their performance on the court; we understand that people do not learn physical skills that way. But do we acknowledge that the same caution applies to how students learn cognitive skills?

Cognitive development theory implies that to motivate students, we must create a match for them between what we want to teach and how and what they are able to learn. It is, therefore, almost futile to write about motivating students and omit a reference to the motivational implications of the way students learn and make sense of the world.

According to theorists such as Piaget (described in Gruber and Voneche, 1977), intellectual development occurs in a series of stages that determine not just what we will learn but also how we will make sense of the world. For example, in simple terms, Piagetian theory has as the highest level of development the ability to engage in abstract theoretical reasoning. However, this stage of thinking does not evolve automatically but instead must be built on a solid foundation of concrete reasoning. Tasks that provide actual experience in the application of concepts to see what works and how, are necessary before students can understand theoretical principles that can then be generalized and applied to other situations. In their first two years of college, most students are functioning at a concrete stage of development with regard to most content. When we try to teach them theory devoid of experience, their learning is superficial, similar to trying to construct tall buildings on a foundation of sand. This result shows up particularly in science courses when students are asked to solve problems. They often try to apply some formula they have memorized. When it does not work, they cannot figure out why. Most often the answer is that they have not really understood the abstractions behind the formula because it has been memorized, rather than understood.

Learning is an active not a passive experience. Students learn by acting on their environments, changing what they experience in order to relate it to what they already know. Memorizing is not learning, and when material is not incorporated into a broad conceptual structure, no understanding occurs and what is memorized is easily forgotten.

Piaget's cognitive development theory and other reformulations of this theory make us aware that (1) the stage a student is at will have a tremendous influence on what will be learned, regardless of what we try to teach and (2) as teachers we have an obligation to provide experiences that help students move along in their development.

Implications for Teaching. The fact that many college students are at a concrete level of cognitive development means that they will have difficulty making any real connections if we begin class by presenting theories, then terminology, followed by definitions of new terms. Unless they understand the concept first, we are providing labels for empty pictures. In behavioral science classes, students often ask questions that relate the topic under discussion to their own lives. In my early days of teaching, I found myself becoming defensive when students said that the concepts I was teaching were wrong because "I have a friend who . . . and that wasn't true." My response was to try to establish for them the methodology of science that allows us to draw conclusions: generation of hypotheses, research designs, control of variables, sampling procedures, and statistical analyses of data. What I was not aware of at the time was that their questions characterized the way their learning was occurring. They were trying to relate what they were being taught to what they already "knew," thus integrating what is new knowledge with what is old and familiar. They were being concrete in their thinking and I was trying to respond to them at a formal level of reasoning. By understanding their attempt to relate what I was teaching to what they already knew, and working within their framework, helping them to figure out why generalizations cannot be drawn on the basis of one experience, I would have been more effective in helping them to learn, and at the same time reducing my own frustration.

In addition to understanding how the stage of development affects learning, we can glean from cognitive development theory the necessity of helping students move along in their development. We have known for some time that material is best learned when it is just above the level at which students are functioning, not too familiar and not too strange. Otherwise, it would not be possible for them to find a match so that they can assimilate what we are trying to teach them. As a matter of fact, a key characteristic of a good teacher is to present material in ways that enable students to find the handle that makes new material accessible. Therefore, understanding the level at which the students are currently functioning and providing concepts or activities that are just above their level, yet still related, helps move them along. We might ask students to give us examples or applications of concepts that are being presented, or, at a higher reasoning level, to analyze, synthesize, and evaluate what is being discussed. We need such feedback, not just at examination time, when it may be too late, but especially while we are teaching.

Another important concept in helping students develop is the premise that they must be actively involved in the material in order to make the connections and revisions implied in development. If we teach simply by lecturing, it is probable that what happens is akin to what happens to children when they go to a booth at a fair and have their faces painted. Bits and pieces of facts and theory will be memorized, learned at a level of rote or even meaningful memory, but not truly integrated, so that no real learning occurs. Students sometimes observe that they have forgotten most of what they learned in a course a few weeks after a semester is over. When a final exam for a course is done, it is as if they have stepped into a shower and washed off what was painted on the surface of their skin. This is because instead of real learning, which integrates new knowledge with what they already know, students have memorized facts without integrating them into broad concepts or structures. No permanent change has occurred in them or in their perspective on a subject.

Research in cognitive psychology, particularly information-processing models of learning (McKeachie, Pintrich, Lin, and Smith, 1986), offers exciting implications for more effective integration of learning. Studies on collaborative or interactive learning and on the teaching of critical thinking strongly demonstrate that the integration of new material with old learning necessarily involves activity. One sure way to prevent learning, kill motivation, and foster dependency is to create passivity in students. Clearly, telling is not teaching, nor does it help students reach a higher stage of development.

What can stimulate active learning in the classroom? Experiential learning—for example, simulations, well-planned small group discussions with carefully structured questions, case studies, role playing, observation and analysis of real phenomena, and many of the other participatory methods of instruction (Frederick, 1989)—requires active learning, which is more likely than passive learning to be integrated with what we know and thus is not soon forgotten. And most of these methods also challenge students to operate at a higher cognitive level than the passive receipt of information characteristic of learning in lectures.

Theory 4: Self-Efficacy Theory

Tenet. Motivation is related to students' beliefs about their abilities for and probabilities of success.

According to this theory, the single most important motivating force for any of us is self-efficacy, that is, our feelings of competence. If performing a given behavior increases our self-efficacy, motivation to engage in it again is strengthened.

Beliefs about one's ability and the explanations one gives oneself for success or failure clearly affect motivation. When high achievers are successful, they explain success in terms of having a high level of ability and exerting strong effort. When high achievers fail or do poorly, the explanation they give themselves for failure is that they did not try hard enough. High achievers, therefore, believe that success or failure is closely related to their actions (amount of effort expended). In other words, they are in control of their lives.

When low achievers succeed, they are likely to explain success in terms of the task being easy or as a matter of luck. When low achievers fail, they believe it is because they do not have as much ability as others who did well, or the task was too hard. This extensively researched personality variable (Rotter, 1966) is a form of expectation—a generalized expectation of control over reinforcement. Internal control refers to the perception or expectation that both positive and negative events are a consequence of one's own behavior and are thus under personal control. External control refers to the perception or expectation that events are independent of one's own behavior and are therefore beyond personal control. In Rotter's theory, the situational expectancy is a function of both a specific expectancy and a generalized expectancy, the latter being modified by previous experience in the situation.

Not only will some students work hard in our classes because they believe that their own efforts will affect their success, others will give up because they feel convinced from past experience that nothing they can do will contribute to success. The concept of learned helplessness (Seligman and Maier, 1967) is basically the learned expectation that one's behavior has no effect on achieving desired outcomes, or that satisfactions or rewards are independent of whatever one does. Experimentally, learned helplessness is engendered by exposing subjects to an uncontrollable, aversive situation that they can neither escape nor solve (Hiroto and Seligman, 1975). (Think of the many classroom experiences on the primary or secondary level in which culturally and economically disadvantaged students do not have the self-esteem or academic skills to cope. What they learn is, "No matter what I do, it doesn't make any difference, so why try?") Subjects exposed to helplessness pretreatments have generally been found to have debilitated performance on subsequent tasks, even when those tasks are controllable (Hiroto and Seligman, 1975; Seligman, 1975). ("Now I am told there are some things I can do to achieve success. But they probably won't make a difference!")

Implications for Teaching. Think about grading and feedback. Grades clearly influence student behavior (Becker, Geer, and Hughes, 1968; Moffett, 1988). From the point of view of cognitive theory, feedback is most useful when it enhances self-efficacy. This alone is an important reason why feedback should be positive, or at least emphasize that although performance on a particular task was not good for certain specific reasons, the instructor believes that this does not represent a student's best effort. Such constructive feedback may gradually increase confidence in students who believe they are not competent and may motivate them to try harder because they begin to see a relationship between effort and performance. This is a good reason for writing comments on papers, not just returning them with a letter or number grade, because such feedback will have an important effect on whether a student feels that increasing effort will pay off.

Theory 5: Expectancy-Value Theory

Tenet. Motivation is the result of an interaction between students' beliefs about themselves and the perceived value of the task.

This most recent model has been used to conceptualize the interactions among motivational, cognitive, and instructional variables (McKeachie, Pintrich, Lin, and Smith, 1986). There are two components to the theory. The first, like self-efficacy theory, is related to students' beliefs about how effort is related to performance and how that in turn affects goal achievement. Thus, students who believe that they have control over outcomes, that is, that trying hard results in good quality work, which in turn leads to goal achievement, will persist longer in studying, completing assignments, and doing well in courses (Pintrich, 1988). However, this is not the complete picture. The second part of the theory requires that we look at how valuable achievement of a particular task is for students and what the students' goals are.

Task value is made up of three components: attainment value, interest value, and utility value. Task value asks how important is it to the student to attain a goal, that is, does a student feel that doing well in a course is a challenge, yet one that can be handled? Interest value refers to whether a student is intrinsically interested in the subject matter, for example, does the student enjoy sociology? Finally, utility value asks whether a student perceives completion of a task useful; for example, a course, such as statistics, which a student might not take if given the choice, has a high utility value because performing statistical analyses of data is necessary if one wants to become a psychologist.

The other aspect of values includes the student's short-term (course or exam) and long-term (life and career) goals. Such goals help determine a student's perception of the value of a task, or, indeed, even the choice of tasks, for example, a student choosing to study Spanish instead of French to increase later employability as a psychologist in New York City. In this model, the interaction of expectancy and value are important determiners of the student's effort and success in college.

Implications for Teaching. Clearly, we need to consider both expectancy and value in designing instruction. Regarding expectancy, one would consider such matters as structuring course material to increase the probability of student success; providing feedback that identifies the positive aspects of a student's work, while pointing out what needs to be done to improve other parts of an assignment; and expressing confidence that additional effort will bring about improvement.

The value portion might suggest deliberate attempts by the instructor to create a challenge, for example, challenging a class by asking questions that push students to think through a problem individually or in small groups. Or, the instructor can appeal to interest value by posing an intriguing problem to be addressed during that class. For utility value, showing how what is being taught can be useful should enhance motivation. How course content can be useful to students is often assumed to be self-evident or left to the students to figure out. However, since such interest affects motivation, it is important that connections and applications be addressed and discovered.

Conclusion

Traditionally, when faculty have thought about preparing for class, they have focused on content. *"What* will I present?" Now, faculty in many institutions are beginning to recognize the importance of teaching style. *"How* will I present and what can I do to motivate my students?"

This chapter has summarized briefly several theories of motivation, explanations of what is happening in the learner that affects motivation, and how instructors can capitalize on such factors. A number of these theories share common concepts, and their applications could look very similar. For example, several theories emphasize the importance of providing positive, rewarding experiences in the classroom; the need for an instructor who is an enthusiastic role model; the value of providing frequent, early positive feedback, which enhances the learners' beliefs that they can successfully accomplish the learning task; and the significance of indicating the ways in which specific learning is useful and can be generalized to other parts of students' lives. Our continuing efforts to understand the implications of these theories and research from the perspective of our own experiences, and to integrate such insights into our teaching, can help us to reframe what we are doing and to generate in ourselves a renewed excitement about teaching, all of which can result in a significant difference in what goes on in the classroom and in how our students are educated.

References

Bandura, A. "Self-Efficacy: Towards a Unifying Theory of Behavior Change." *Psychological Review*, 1977a, *84,* 191–215.

Bandura, A. *Social Learning Theory.* Englewood Cliffs, N.J.: Prentice Hall, 1977b.

Bandura, A., and Walters, R. H. *Social Learning and Personality Development.* New York: Holt, Rinehart & Winston, 1963.

Becker, H. S., Geer, B., and Hughes, E. C. *Making the Grade: The Academic Side of College Life.* New York: Wiley, 1968.

Chickering, A., and Associates (eds.). *The Modern American College: Responding to the New Realities of Diverse Students and a Changing Society.* San Francisco: Jossey-Bass, 1981.

Ericksen, S. C. *The Essence of Good Teaching: Helping Students Learn and Remember What They Learn.* San Francisco: Jossey-Bass, 1984.

Frederick, P. J. "Involving Students More Actively in the Classroom." In A. Lucas (ed.), *The Department Chairperson's Role in Enhancing College Teaching.* New Directions for Teaching and Learning, no. 37. San Francisco: Jossey-Bass, 1989.

Gruber, H. E., and Voneche, J. J. (eds.). *The Essential Piaget: An Interpretative Reference and Guide.* New York: Basic Books, 1977.

Hiroto, D. S., and Seligman, M. P. "Generality of Learned Helplessness in Man." *Journal of Personality and Social Psychology*, 1975, *31*, 311–327.

McKeachie, W. "The Decline and Fall of the Laws of Learning." *Educational Researcher*, 1974, *3*, 7–11.

McKeachie, W., Pintrich, P. R., Lin, Y., and Smith, D. *Teaching and Learning in the College Classroom: A Review of the Research Literature.* Ann Arbor: National Center for Research to Improve Postsecondary Teaching and Learning, University of Michigan, 1986.

Moffet, M. *Coming of Age in New Jersey.* New Brunswick, N.J.: Rutgers University Press, 1988.

Newman, J. H. *The Idea of a University.* Westminster, Md.: Christian Classics, 1973. (Originally published 1852.)

Pintrich, P. R. "A Process-Oriented View of Student Motivation and Cognition." In J. S. Stark and L. A. Mets (eds.), *Improving Teaching and Learning Through Research.* New Directions for Institutional Research, no. 54. San Francisco: Jossey-Bass, 1988.

Rotter, J. "Generalized Expectancies of Internal Versus External Control of Reinforcement." *Psychological Monographs*, 1966, *80* (entire issue 609).

Seligman, M. *Helplessness: On Depression, Development, and Death.* San Francisco: W. H. Freeman, 1975.

Seligman, M., and Maier, A. D. "Failure to Escape Traumatic Shock." *Journal of Experimental Psychology*, 1967, *74*, 1–9.

Ann F. Lucas is a licensed psychologist and professor and campus chair of the Department of Management at Fairleigh Dickinson University, Teaneck, New Jersey. Her book The Department Chairperson's Role in Enhancing College Teaching *was published by Jossey-Bass in 1989.*

PART THREE

What Next?

Faculty, like all other professionals, should be conscious of the need for continuing education in teaching as well as in mastery of their disciplines. This chapter lists some resources to help them keep up-to-date.

"Study" Your Way to Better Teaching

Maryellen Weimer

High on the agenda for faculty in the 1990s is the cultivation of lifelong learning skills. The issue of skills was raised in the 1970s, endorsed in the 1980s, and, one hopes, will be acted on in the 1990s. As faculty work with students to foster a commitment to learning and a recognition that formal education begins (not ends) the quest for knowledge, faculty members themselves must heed the lessons they are teaching. Most are by nature inquisitive, curious, independent, and lifelong learners when it comes to continuing their own education in their respective disciplines, but few "study" teaching with the same commitment and spirit of inquiry. However, as national attention is focused on college teaching and the need to improve teaching begins to be taken more seriously by institutions and individuals, faculty in the 1990s should begin to think of teaching as a phenomenon worth continued study and reflection.

For too long faculty and others in the higher-education community have assumed, "If you know it, you can teach it." From this perspective, teaching is not a phenomenon or entity in its own right but merely a function subsumed in the knowledge of the content. To propose that faculty direct scholarly attention to teaching is to view the activity as a phenomenon of substance and complexity, worthy of serious intellectual thought and reflection. It is also to recognize that not all of the variables of teaching are clearly understood. How they interact and with what effect in the classroom of the individual instructor is difficult to predict. Finally, recognition of the ongoing nature of learning about teaching entails acknowledgment that instructional skills cannot be "canned" or otherwise preserved and then opened as they are needed across a teaching career. Rather, teaching skills need continued attention, refinement, and readjustment as teachers, students, and content change over time and circumstances.

Will Studying Teaching Have Any Effect?

If teaching does become the object of greater scholarly attention, will it improve? Assume a faculty member decides to regularly access resources about teaching, will that affect how that individual teaches? Will the effect be positive? Since few faculty currently attempt to "learn" about teaching in systematic ways and since no research known to the author assesses the effectiveness of these attempts, the answer is based on conjecture, but there are sound reasons why teaching should improve. Consider four.

First, most of the literature on teaching tends to be *applied* rather than *theoretical*. It is written by practitioners who describe instructional dilemmas they know or have experienced. They write to describe the problem, but also, and more importantly, to share solutions, what they have tried and how it works. Certainly, some literature on teaching explores philosophical perspectives and conceptual orientations and, certainly, faculty ought to be reading that material as well. But, on the whole, what faculty will find to read about teaching emphasizes the practical: ideas, strategies, techniques, policies, and practices that can be tried in class tomorrow. The literature lends itself to further application. Consequently, the "study" of teaching in this literature facilitates instructional change.

Second, a systematic study of teaching via the resources available today will infuse instruction with *a steady supply of fresh ideas*. Here the improvement may not result so much from the study as from alteration of the fact that faculty who teach today and those being prepared to teach in colleges and universities tomorrow typically receive few, if any, instructions on how to teach. Most faculty begin and continue careers in teaching with limited instructional repertoires. Because the literature on teaching tends to be practical, it is filled with ideas, most of which are not revolutionary but are at least innovative to instructors who have never used them. Many faculty use the same old tried-and-true techniques year after year because they do not know others exist. To read about teaching is to infuse the activity with new ideas and possibilities. Teaching will improve if nourished by new, rich ideas.

Third, reading about and systematically studying the craft of teaching improve instruction because they *force reflection*. The problem with many faculty is that they teach unaware of *how* they teach. Even the very mechanical aspects of teaching such as where the instructors stand in the classroom, to what part of the room they direct questions, when they ask questions, and how they handle answers to questions escape their conscious awareness. As often as faculty complete those tasks, many are hard pressed to describe accurately their teaching behaviors. Even fewer can offer any sort of rationale as to why they handle the mechanical and procedural aspects of teaching as they do. Given the lack of preparation to teach and lack of attention most faculty direct toward their teaching, their instructional unawareness (though regrettable) is not surprising. Scholarly materials confront faculty and their individual practices in the light of what others propose. They are encouraged to think about and observe their teaching policies and practices.

Finally, reading and study improve instruction because they *inspire instructors.* Faculty members need inspiration? They do indeed. For far too long the psychologically draining aspects of teaching have been repressed and ignored. Effective instruction requires teachers to give, often more than they receive. In many cases they have been expected to give in institutional climates where the value and merit of their contributions are not appreciated. Teacher burn-out is a fact of life on many college and university campuses, but like other social diseases, this one is rarely discussed, and those who suffer from it are often the last to admit they have a problem. A commitment to instructional study will probably not cure the disease in its advanced stages, but it can be preventive medicine and does have curative powers for faculty who are beginning to feel tired and uninspired. The literature on teaching contains positive affirmations of the value and potential of the activity, as well as some powerful descriptions of the joys and sorrows of the profession. Classroom performance is the first to benefit when faculty touch these softer spots of the profession, when their commitments to teaching are renewed and revitalized.

Maximizing the Impact of Studying Teaching

Individual reading and study do have the potential to improve instruction. But they are not without caveats. They only result in better teaching if faculty *do* something about what they have read. An article may contain twenty-five good ideas for encouraging student participation, but unless the instructor decides to use the ideas, they will have no effect on instructional quality. The practical, applied nature of the literature helps to overcome this limitation, but faculty need to know that action is an essential component of instructional study. Articles on teaching should never be read without the simultaneous preparation of a "to-do" list that outlines proposed actions to be taken as a result of the reading. Maybe the article requires no classroom action, but it may need to be shared with a colleague or filed for future reference. Whatever the action, instructional study should not occur without it.

Second, the improvement of instruction through self-study is limited to the extent that faculty do not make it a regular and systematic part of their professional lives. Much like exercise where an occasional work-out has limited (if any) effect on overall fitness, a haphazard, occasional study of teaching has little or no effect on overall instructional quality. It is at this juncture that significant attitudinal adjustments need to occur. Faculty have many pressures on their time and, given past and present climates for teaching on many campuses, are not inclined to add still more to their work loads. Moreover, because of long-prevalent attitudes toward teaching, there is a tendency to regard its improvement as some-thing that can be done quickly and easily as long as the right remedy is used. Faculty tend to look for quick fixes and sure-fire solutions, which in reality do not fix or solve significant problems of teaching. Good teaching skills develop slowly and in nine cases out of ten are the result of concerted and sustained effort. Because good teaching skills develop this way, the notion of "studying" one's way to better teaching accurately describes the desired response to resources on teaching and learning.

Resources on teaching and learning do exist but not all of them are found in readily accessible journals and in organized and catalogued col-lections. Rather, instructional resources are widely dispersed across a broad spectrum of higher education literature. Only one point is certain: most are outside the confines of any individual discipline. This means faculty with limited time will have to spend part of it tracking down unfamiliar resources, which makes resource listings like those in this chapter necessary and valuable.

Adding to the difficulty of accessing resources on teaching and learn-ing are the formats. Some very valuable resources are not formatted as books or journals. They are newsletters, occasionally published papers, handbooks (done in three-ring spiral notebooks), guidebooks, source-books, bulletins, and magazines, to name some of the more common. Libraries do well collecting and indexing conventional materials; they do less well with these alternative resources.

The location and nature of these teaching-learning resources speaks eloquently for additional institutional effort to assemble and otherwise make accessible a special collection of teaching-learning materials for faculty. Whether those materials are housed in the main library, are the responsibility of a teaching-excellence center, or are looked after by an administrator depends on the nature of the institution. The first require-ment, however, is an institutional effort to support faculty interest in learning more about teaching. In the absence of that institutional com-mitment, concerned faculty may need to ban together and lobby for the necessary resources and support. If an institution cares about instruc-tional quality, it ought to care enough to make materials available to faculty. After all, the improvement of teaching by self-study is one of the more economical approaches to instructional development.

The resource lists to follow are not meant to be comprehensive but rather only illustrative of the kind and location of resources on teaching and learning. Moreover, no attempt has been made to assemble any sort of definitive or best collection of resources. Certainly, materials of dubious value do not appear in the collection, but not everything of substantive value appears here either. The list illustrates what faculty in the 1990s might study to further develop instructional effectiveness.

The resources are divided into three major categories: books, journals, and other material (including the alternative types of resources mentioned previously). Each of these categories begins with observations about the nature of the resources in the area and advice on an appropriate "diet" for faculty about to embark on a healthy, instructional, self-study program.

Books

A variety of different books on teaching do exist, although most have never been on best-seller lists, nor are they venerated texts. In addition to books devoted exclusively to teaching are books that cover an aspect or dimension of the larger teaching task. There is also a group of books that explores teaching in a larger, more philosophical context or that elaborates another phenomenon (like motivation, for example) with direct implications for teaching. There are a few books that report and summarize research findings with instructional implications. Most of these cannot be recommended to faculty. They are written for researchers interested in pursuing related research topics. A few notable exceptions do exist. Finally, there is a small group of "classics," books on teaching that have withstood the test of time and are still widely read and very often quoted in current literature.

Busy faculty who elect to do some instructional reading and study tend to choose first the books on technique. Publishers have figured this out, which explains why so many of the books on teaching fall into this category. Books that address the technical aspects of instruction have the highest payoff because they propose alternative ideas, strategies, techniques, policies, and approaches. Potentially, they can change what happens in class tomorrow. Moreover, books that offer suggestions on how to teach tend to be well organized. They divide the topic into component parts and cover each part independently. This too appeals to busy faculty. They can elect to read first or exclusively those parts of the books with immediate interest or relevance to them. These are the books that can be picked up for reading across a period of time with little or no need to review. This feature appeals to college teachers who seldom have the luxury of reading a book in one or two sittings.

And faculty members should read books in this category. But they should read books in other categories as well. Books covering an aspect of teaching force in-depth analysis and reflection. Books exploring teaching from a more theoretical/experiential perspective do not have the immediate next-day payoffs. Their effects are more indirect, but probably also more enduring and substantive, than technical books. They beg to be discussed by presenting ideas and reactions for exchanges, debates, and exploration in the context of a particular discipline. To the extent these books stimulate the exchange and refinement of ideas about teaching, they increase still further their potential to influence instruction.

Technique (as in How to Teach) Books
Beard, R. M., and Hartley, J. *Teaching and Learning in Higher Education.* (4th ed.) New York: Harper & Row, 1984.

Eble, K. E. *The Craft of Teaching: A Guide to Mastering the Professor's Art.* (2nd ed.) San Francisco: Jossey-Bass, 1988.

Ericksen, S. C. *The Essence of Good Teaching: Helping Students Learn and Remember What They Learn.* San Francisco: Jossey-Bass, 1984.

Fuhrmann, B. S., and Grasha, A. F. *Handbook for College Teachers.* Boston: Little, Brown, 1983.

Lowman, J. *Mastering the Techniques of Teaching.* San Francisco: Jossey-Bass, 1984.

Books on Aspects of Instruction
Boud, D. (ed.). *Developing Student Autonomy in Learning.* (2nd ed.) London and New York: Kogan Page and Nichols, 1988.

Christensen, C. R. *Teaching and the Case Method.* Cambridge, Mass.: Harvard Business School, 1987.

Cross, K. P. *Adults as Learners: Increasing Participation and Facilitating Learning.* San Francisco: Jossey-Bass, 1981.

Books on Teaching from a Philosophical, Theoretical, or Experiential Point of View; or Philosophical, Theoretical, and Experiential Books with Significant Implications for Teaching
Cahn, S. (ed.). *Scholars Who Teach.* Chicago: Nelson-Hall, 1978.

Eisner, E. W. *The Educational Imagination.* (2nd ed.) New York: Macmillan, 1985.

Epstein, J. (ed.). *Masters: Portraits of Great Teachers.* New York: Basic Books, 1981.

Freire, P. *Pedagogy of the Oppressed.* New York: Herder and Herder, 1970.

Giamatti, A. B. *A Free and Ordered Space.* New York: W. W. Norton, 1988.

Knapper, C. K., and Cropley, A. J. *Lifelong Learning and Higher Education.* Dover, N.H.: Croom Helm, 1985.

Kohl, H. *Growing Minds: On Becoming a Teacher.* New York: Harper & Row, 1984.

Kohn, A. *No Contest: The Case Against Competition.* Boston: Houghton Mifflin, 1986.

Schön, D. A. *The Reflective Practitioner.* New York: Books, 1984.

Books Reporting Relevant Research
Dewey, J. *How We Think.* Boston: D. C. Heath, 1983.

McKeachie, W. J. *Teaching Tips: A Guidebook for the Beginning College Teacher.* (8th ed.) Lexington, Mass.: D. C. Heath, 1986.

Whitehead, A. N. *The Aims of Education and Other Essays.* New York: Macmillan, 1969.

General Reference Book Pointing Toward Further Reading
Menges, R., and Mathis, B. C. *Key Readings on Teaching, Learning, Curriculum, and Faculty Development: A Guide to the Higher Education Literature.* San Francisco: Jossey-Bass, 1988.

Journals

Given the time constraints under which most faculty operate, it is reasonable to expect them to read more journals than books, or at least to read journals more regularly than books. The problem with material on teaching and learning in journals is that it appears in so many different publications. To date, only two journals are devoted to college teaching independently of an academic discipline context. One of these is a long-standing publication; the other is an established journal but with a new focus on college teaching. These are the only journals on teaching that faculty should read regularly and to which they can justifiably subscribe.

However, these two journals do not publish everything faculty need to study teaching. Other excellent materials appear occasionally in a variety of educational journals that are not exclusively devoted to college teaching. It is unrealistic to expect faculty members to regularly read all of these journals, and it is probably equally unrealistic to expect them to peruse the publications even intermittently. For these reasons, a study program works best if someone other than a faculty member at the institution regularly reviews the publications, identifying relevant articles on teaching and learning. In the absence of such a person, faculty may need to organize themselves, assigning different journals to different individuals. However access to these journals is organized, time limitations are and will continue to be a major hurdle that those interested in instructional study need to overcome.

A number of academic disciplines have their own pedagogical publications. Unfortunately, many of these journals are not well read within the discipline, to say nothing of not being read at all by others outside the field. This is unfortunate because, although these journals do vary in quality, if they were more widely read, if publications in them were counted at promotion and tenure time, the quality would undoubtedly improve. Faculty interested in teaching scholarship should certainly read the discipline-specific journal of their fields, or of related fields if no journal exists in their academic specialty. Faculty should also read (again intermittently, but still regularly) pedagogical publications outside of their fields. A review of these publications illustrates how many instructional concerns transcend disciplines. Many times the issue is treated generically enough to be of interest and value to faculty in other disciplines. The list of resources here identifies a few of the many articles in discipline-specific journals with broad-based faculty appeal.

Finally, the list of journal resources does not include research articles. Many exist, but few can be recommended for general faculty reading. A few notable exceptions occur (some are included in the list of articles from journals not exclusively devoted to college teaching). These are exceptions in that the articles do not emphasize methodological issues, they are written in language that does not presume familiarity with a technical research vocabulary, and they discuss the instructional implications of the findings, that is, what the results mean in terms of instructional practice.

The difficulty in deciphering research findings, however, does not excuse faculty from knowing what the research has documented about teaching and learning. For far too long faculty have taught unaware that many important instructional issues have been addressed empirically. Some findings are definitive enough to have instructional implications that ought to affect practicing professionals. The gap between research and practice can be blamed on poor communication from both sides. Efforts to bridge the gap deserve commendation. Consider two examples.

In 1965 the U.S. Office of Education created the Educational Resources Information Center, or ERIC as it is more commonly called, to transmit the findings of current educational research to teachers, administrators, researchers, and the public. ERIC accomplishes its goals by publishing Resources in Education and Current Index to Journals in Education. Together these two publications make it possible for faculty to search a vast data base and easily assemble a bibliography of research resources on almost any topic of interest and relevance. ERIC does not make reading the research any easier, but it does aid tremendously in organizing and accessing it.

In 1986 a U.S. Department of Education grant helped to establish the National Center for Research to Improve Postsecondary Teaching and Learning (NCRIPTAL) at the University of Michigan. Grant support enables researchers studying five key areas of higher education to share findings with educators, administrators, policymakers, and the general public. They do so in a family of publications, modestly priced and available from NCRIPTAL, 2400 School of Education Building, University of Michigan, Ann Arbor, Michigan 48109. Of particular value to faculty interested in better teaching are *Teaching and Learning in the College Classroom: A Review of the Research Literature*, W. J. McKeachie and others (1986); *Classroom Assessment Techniques: A Handbook for Faculty*, K. P. Cross and T. A. Angelo (1988); and *Planning Introductory College Courses: Influences on Faculty*, J. S. Stark and others (forthcoming).

Journals on College Teaching to Be Read Regularly
College Teaching, HELDREF Publications, 4000 Albemarle St., N.W., Washington, D.C. 20016.

Journal of Professional Studies, Faculty Center for Instructional Effectiveness, Eastern Michigan University, Ypsilanti, Michigan 48197.

Journals Not Exclusively on College Teaching, but with an Occasional Good Article
Educational Forum; for example, R. L. Weaver, "The Small Group in Large Classes," 1983, *48* (1), 65–73.

Educational Leadership; for example, E. Eisner, "The Art and Craft of Teaching," 1983, *40* (4), 5–13.

Harvard Educational Review, particularly the feature "About Teachers and Teaching" and the book review section; for example, W. Ayers, "Thinking About Teachers and the Curriculum," 1986, *56* (1), 49–51; and D. Meier, "Learning in Small Moments," 1986, *56* (3), 298–300.

Instructional Science; for example, K. A. Kiewra, "Notetaking and Review: The Research and Its Implications," 1987, *16* (3), 233–249.

126   THE CHANGING FACE OF COLLEGE TEACHING

Journal of College Student Personnel; for example, D. C. Barnett and J. C. Dalton, "Why College Students Cheat," 1981, *22* (6), 545-551.

Journal of Higher Education, particularly the book review section; for example, W. C. Williams, "Effective Teaching: Gauging Learning While Teaching," 1985, *56* (3), 320-337.

Journal of Instructional Development; for example, C. A. Carrier, "Note-taking Research: Implication for the Classroom," 1983, *6* (3), 19-25.

Performance and Instruction; for example, S. Yelon, and M. Massa, "Heuristics for Creating Examples," 1987, *26* (8), 13-16.

Phi Delta Kappan; for example, J. S. Rigden, "The Art of Great Science," 1983, *64* (9), 53-59.

Studies in Higher Education; for example, D. Fox, "Personal Theories of Teaching," 1983, *8* (20), 151-163; and J. P. Powell, and L. W. Andersen, "Humor and Teaching in Higher Education," 1985, *10* (1), 79-88.

**Sampling of Discipline-Specific Pedagogical Journals with
Articles Relevant to All Teachers**
Association of Departments of English Bulletin; for example, R. W. Hanning, "The Classroom as Theatre of Self: Some Observations for Beginning Teachers," 1984, *77,* 33-37.

Engineering Education; for example, K. A. Kiewra, "Memory Compatible Instruction," 1987, *77* (5), 285-290.

Journal of Chemical Education; for example, D. W. Brooks, "Alternatives to Traditional Lecturing," 1984, *61* (10), 858-959.

Journal of College Science Teaching; for example, B. C. Pestel, "Some Practical Distinctions Between Preaching, Teaching and Training," 1988, *18* (1), 26-31.

Organizational Behavior Teaching Review; for example, W. Ewens, "Teaching Using Discussion," 1985-1986, *10* (3), 77-80; and J. Harvey, "Encouraging Students to Cheat: One Thought on the Difference Between Teaching Ethics and Teaching Ethically," 1984, *9* (2), 1-13.

Teaching Psychology; for example, L. Barker, and B. R. Lombardi, "Students' Lecture Notes and Their Relation to Test Performance," 1985, *12* (1), 28-32.

Teaching Sociology; for example, J. Billson, "The College Classroom as a Small Group: Some Implications for Teaching and Learning," 1986, *14*, 143–151.

Other Material

In addition to the conventional resources on teaching, there exists a large and eclectic collection of "other" materials. What is included in this collection? Begin with what is *not* included: the staples of most faculty reading diets, books and journals. Rather, in this collection are workbooks, handbooks, sourcebooks, and guidebooks; that is, materials formatted to offer easy access to materials and designed to encourage reader interaction with the content. Sometimes there are forms to fill out, worksheets to assemble, study questions to consider, or materials to be taken from the publications and used in class (for example, sample evaluation forms, checklists, and collaborative activities). In general these materials focus on practical instructional details.

Also within this miscellaneous category are several serial publications that either exclusively devote all issues to college teaching or regularly devote individual issues to instructional matters. These publication series combine book and journal elements. They address topics at length, with each issue devoted exclusively to consideration of one topic. They end up being short books. Like journals, they can be purchased by subscription; like books, single issues can be purchased. Authorship/editorship of the individual issues in the series changes.

A certain number of magazines, newspapers, and bulletins also intermittently, but with some degree of regularity, address instructional concerns. Again, busy faculty members probably cannot be expected to review these publications regularly. But faculty members themselves and certainly those working with them in support of good teaching need to be aware of the valuable resources included in these publications.

Finally, in the collection are a group of short, but regular, publications best described as newsletters or paper series. Most of these are sold to subscribers; some are free. The ones identified in the resource collection are devoted exclusively to teaching and learning in higher education.

Resources identified in this final category exemplify a peculiar irony. Unlike books and journals which require substantial commitments of time and energy to glean their resources, many of these materials are designed for easy access, fit comfortably into the busy, frequently interrupted schedules of so many faculty members, and emphasize the practical issues associated with instruction. However, unlike books and journals, which are easily collected, catalogued, and located in libraries where faculty can find them, these materials contribute to faculty instructional knowledge much less regularly because faculty remain unaware of their existence. The nature of these materials demonstrates well the need for bibliographies devoted to organizing the literature and the value of having someone assigned to review these potential sources and make those with relevance and importance available to faculty.

Workbooks, Sourcebooks, Handbooks, and Guidebooks
Allen, R. R., and Rueter, T. *Teaching Assistant Strategies: An Introduction to College Teaching*. Dubuque, Iowa: Kendall/Hunt, 1990.

Bergquist, W. H., and Phillips, S. R. *A Handbook for Faculty Development*. Vols. 1–3. Washington, D.C.: The Council for the Advancement of Small Colleges, 1975, 1977, 1981.

Neff, R. A., and Weimer, M. *Classroom Communication: Collected Readings for Effective Discussion and Questioning*. Madison, Wis.: Magna, 1989.

Weimer, M., Parrett, J. L., and Kerns, M. M. *How Am I Teaching? Forms and Activities for Acquiring Instructional Input*. Madison, Wis.: Magna, 1988.

Series Devoted to College Teaching and Series on Higher Education with Occasional Issues Devoted to College Teaching
New Directions for Teaching and Learning, published quarterly by Jossey-Bass. The series editor identifies current topics of concern and importance to college educators and appoints a sourcebook editor, knowledgeable in the area, who invites individuals with relevant expertise to prepare chapters. Content focuses on practice; sourcebooks in the series frequently introduce new ideas and issues to higher education. With over forty sourcebooks in the series, topics already addressed include *Teaching Writing in All Disciplines* (no. 12), *Learning in Groups* (no. 14), *Rejuvenating Introductory Courses* (no. 20), *Using Research to Improve Teaching* (no. 23), *Distinguished Teachers on Effective Teaching* (no. 28), *Developing Critical Thinking and Problem-Solving Abilities* (no. 30), and *Assessing Students' Learning* (no. 34).

ASHE-ERIC Higher Education Reports, prepared by ERIC, Clearinghouse on Higher Education and published by the Association for the Study of Higher Education. Each monograph, authored by an expert in the area of higher education, offers a thorough analysis of a problem based on review of relevant literature and the experience of institutions. Recent reports devoted to instructional topics include *Learning Styles and Implication for Improving Educational Practices,* no. 4, C. Claxton, and P. H. Murrell (1987); *Critical Thinking: Research, Practice and Possibilities,* no. 2, J. G. Kurfiss (1988); *Peer Teaching: To Teach Is to Learn Twice,* no. 4, N. A. Whitman (1988); and *Increasing Students' Learning: A Faculty Guide to Reducing Stress Among Students,* no. 4, N. A. Whitman, D. C. Spendlove, and C. H. Clark (1986).

Magazines, Newspapers, and Bulletins

American Association of Higher Education Bulletin; for example, W. R. Whipple, "Collaborative Learning: Recognizing It When We See It," October 1987, 3-5.

Change Magazine; for example, K. P. Cross, "Dealing with Diversity: The Challenge of Teaching Today," September 1983, 20-23, 44; M. M. Gullett, "The Heart of Good Teaching," July-August 1984, 8-11, 48; and W. M. Welty, "Discussion Method Teaching," July-August 1989, 41-49.

Chronicle of Higher Education, particularly the end paper feature; for example, J. J. Chiodo, "The Effects on Exam Anxiety of Grandma's Health," August 6, 1986; S. Coady, "Student Irresponsibility: We Helped Cause It," July 6, 1983; N. K. Hill, "Scaling the Heights: The Teacher as Mountaineer," June 16, 1980; and S. Rubin, "Professors, Students and the Syllabus," August 7, 1985.

Training Magazine; for example, M. Broadwell, "It's So Technical I Have to Lecture," March 1989, 41-44.

Newsletters and Paper Series

IDEA Papers; Center for Faculty Evaluation and Development, Kansas State University, Manhattan, Kansas 66502. The twenty-one papers in this series, all four to eight pages in length, address instructional issues such as *Questioning in the College Classroom* (no. 8), *Improving Lectures* (no. 14), *Improving Discussions* (no. 15), *Improving Essay Tests* (no. 17), and *Improving College Grading* (no. 19).

Innovation Abstracts; National Institute for Staff and Organizational Development, University of Texas, EDB 348, Austin, Texas 78712. This two-page paper is issued weekly when classes are in session and reports on new, novel, and innovative approaches to various aspects of instruction.

Teaching Excellence; Professional and Organizational Development Network in Higher Education, Teaching/Learning Center, University of

Nebraska, Lincoln, Nebraska 68588. This two-page thought piece is issued eight times during the academic year and deals with the more thought-provoking aspects of teaching in higher education.

The Teaching Professor; Magna Publications, 2718 Dryden Drive, Madison, Wisconsin 53704. This monthly (during the academic year) six- to eight-page newsletter addresses a variety of teaching and learning topics in any given issue. It is written to encourage and inform faculty efforts to teach effectively.

*Maryellen Weimer is director of the Instructional
Development Program at The Pennsylvania State University,
University Park.*

Index

ORDERING INFORMATION

NEW DIRECTIONS FOR TEACHING AND LEARNING is a series of paperback books that presents ideas and techniques for improving college teaching, based both on the practical expertise of seasoned instructors and on the latest research findings of educational and psychological researchers. Books in the series are published quarterly in Fall, Winter, Spring, and Summer and are available for purchase by subscription as well as by single copy.

SUBSCRIPTIONS for 1990 cost $39.00 for individuals (a savings of 20 percent over single-copy prices) and $52.00 for institutions, agencies, and libraries. Please do not send institutional checks for personal subscriptions. Standing orders are accepted.

SINGLE COPIES cost $12.95 when payment accompanies order. (California, New Jersey, New York, and Washington, D.C., residents please include appropriate sales tax.) Billed orders will be charged postage and handling.

DISCOUNTS FOR QUANTITY ORDERS are available. Please write to the address below for information.

ALL ORDERS must include either the name of an individual or an official purchase order number. Please submit your order as follows:
   Subscriptions: specify series and year subscription is to begin
   Single copies: include individual title code (such as TL1)

MAIL ALL ORDERS TO:
   Jossey-Bass Inc., Publishers
   350 Sansome Street
   San Francisco, California 94104